VISHNU'S MOUNT

VISHNU'S MOUNT

BIRDS IN INDIAN MYTHOLOGY AND FOLKLORE

CAPT. PRAVEEN CHOPRA

ILLUSTRATIONS
BY
AKASH KUMAR

Notion Press

Old No. 38, New No. 6
McNichols Road, Chetpet
Chennai - 600 031

First Published by Notion Press 2017
Copyright © Praveen Chopra 2017
All Rights Reserved.

ISBN
Hardcase 978-1-948352-68-0
Paperback 978-1-948352-96-3

To my

Parents;

Kiran, my wife;

and

Anjali, Sandeep,

Akshay, Aarti, Sonia,

Sara and Arjun, my ever-loving children

Contents

PART I
MYTHICAL BIRDS

PART II
COMMON BIRDS

Contents

PREFACE

Dual interests in both mythology and birds often sent me scurrying to pundits who could enlighten me on the two diverse subjects with equal dexterity. Long marathon sessions with friends and masters would leave me wondering about the deep influence that birds have on civilisations and cultures across the world, and more so in the Indian context.

Birds are a common part of Indian folklore, music and literature and are frequently anthropomorphised* and linked to deities as their mounts in Indian mythology. Our seers projected them in a supernatural manner, probably with a sense to convey a deep philosophical message about them. There is a missing link between how our seers saw birds during their times and how we see them today in scientific, economic and ecological terms. These two perceptions have been bridged and presented in today's context for better understanding.

For a generalist, the subject was too serious to be delved into and had to be simplified for easy assimilation. As I went fishing for more content, I realised that it was too scattered for my comfort and I felt the need to compile the available knowledge and piece it together under one cover. The resultant effort is not purported to be a research paper. It must, instead, be seen as an effort to discover the wonderful world of mythology and birds in a combined and holistic manner.

Readers may come across some words or terms that they may not be familiar with. A comprehensive glossary of these terms has been included at the end of the book for the readers' convenience. These words can be identified by the asterisk that accompanies them.

FOREWORD

Praveen Chopra is a naturalist, avid bird-watcher, photographer, conservationist and freelance writer who spends as many mornings as he can spare in open spaces, often trekking and observing birds along the Ganga's marshy banks through which the river has meandered in earlier years. He mourns the shrinking bird population and the thoughtless massacres that they are subjected to by greedy hunters who do not think twice about poisoning the waters on which they alight and in which they frolic. His enthusiasm, however, does not diminish for long. A rare sighting, the glimpse of a breeding pair or a nest that promises future delights him. The fact that some homes in Kanpur, a generally inhospitable city for birds, remain filled with dozens of sparrows are always enough to raise his hopes. Indeed, Praveen is a remarkable person.

Praveen is even more unusual because he looks for birds not only in trees and marshlands but also in books, myths and Indian epics. It is this passion that has inspired this book that he has written and which you, the reader, are about to immerse yourself in. It is a fascinating journey that you will embark upon, on the wings of Lakshmi's owl, Murugan's mayura and Vishnu's garuda amongst others. I have made some forays on this journey, and I can vouch for many magical moments during its course.

Praveen has made a tremendous effort to bring together references to birds in the *Puranas*, in the Jataka tales and in various versions of Indian epics. He has found parallels between birds that are familiar to all of us and those that have been endowed with magical properties that enable them to perform heroic deeds in mythology. It was a bird that led Hanuman to Sita in the enclosed garden in Ravana's palace; it was a bird that told Rama about Sita's abduction; it was a bird that stole *amrita* from the gods in order to appease the snakes who were torturing its mother; and, it was the same bird that avenged his mother by killing many of the snakes. There are many, many more wonderful tales and legends that the bird lover in Praveen has laboured for years to uncover and finally compile in a book that is lucid and insightful.

For many people, birds and animals that are the *vahanas* (mounts or the vehicles) of a host of gods and goddesses in Hindu mythology have themselves become objects of worship and veneration. This is despite the fact that not many attempt to reason why a particular bird or animal has been associated with a particular deity. His book *Vishnu's Mount* delves into these questions. Praveen relies not only on the explanations that he has painstakingly gleaned from a range of references but also on his own knowledge of ornithology and the habits of birds that he has himself studied and watched so intimately.

The earliest bird watchers and bird lovers in our country were its earliest inhabitants, mostly tribal people belonging to various tribes and clans within tribes. All across the world, tribals and indigenous people have venerated and protected nature – forests, birds and animals – despite the fact that they have been dependent on these for food, clothing, weapons and shelter. Aware of the value of their natural habitat and of its fragility and vulnerability, they hunted and utilised with caution and consideration what the forests and wild plains made available to them in abundance. Most tribes associated themselves with one particular bird or animal – their totem* – which they did not hunt or eat. Perhaps this was a primitive form of conservation.

This veneration of totem birds and animals has continued until the modern period and is well recorded. For example, the Santal *(Santhal)* tribals living in the Eastern part of the country believe that the two earliest living beings were a heavenly bird couple – *Has and Hasil* (Goose and Gander) – whom God created from his hair. After flying between heaven and earth for some time, they built a nest and laid eggs. The first male human, *Pilchu Haram,* and female human, *Pilchu Burhi,* emerged out of these eggs. In this way, the pair of birds Has and Hasil was credited with the creation of the human race. Many tribal clans were their progeny, and the one with the highest status was the Hansdak clan whose members claim direct descent from *Has* (wild goose or swan). *Dak* means water and refers to the nest that their bird ancestors built on the water that covered the earth at the beginning of time.

The clan that is second in importance is the Murmu clan that has the antelope as its totem. The third is the Kisku clan that has the kingfisher as its totem and is of royal status.

All the clans were devoted to their totem animals and birds and thought of them as their clan members. If they found their totem bird (or animal) dead, they observed funeral rituals in their honour.

Over time, the tribals were displaced from their primacy in most parts of the country by agricultural settlers with different gods. The vahanas may be telling us the story of this displacement in ways that have still not been completely understood or accepted, and it is very likely that the vahanas actually represent the tribes for whom they were the totem. Their becoming the vehicles of various gods and goddesses may be a depiction of the vanquishing of a tribe by the worshippers of a particular deity. At the same time, the fact that the vahanas continue to be venerated or worshipped by the victors maybe a tribute to the bravery of the vanquished tribals and a mark of respect for their beliefs.

Surely, we need to treat these birds and animals with respect, these vahanas that we continue to worship and venerate with the kindness and consideration that our tribal ancestors did and our tribal brothers and sisters continue to do even today. I am sure that Praveen not only empathises with these tribal sentiments but is doing whatever he can to promote them. The devotion with which he has written this book and brought to light so many aspects of our heritage and the important place that birds occupy in our folklore should inspire all of us, his readers, to not only appreciate what he is sharing with us but to respond to the heartfelt plea that is not seen but can be felt on every page of his book to treat birds with both awe and love. The cruelty that is often inflicted on them must inspire horror and opposition.

Readers of this book will certainly enjoy every page of it. I am sure it will inspire many to enter the wonderful and inspirational world of bird-watching, bird-studying and bird-loving. And for that, they will thank Praveen for the rest of their lives.

Subhashini Ali,

Former Member of Parliament

ACKNOWLEDGEMENTS

Thank you, Mum and Dad, for being the kindly light that leads me. This book would have never happened without your divine presence.

Kiran, I am indebted to you for being such a delightful companion and for having allowed me to pen this book, sometimes late into the wintry nights, without ever complaining.

Sandeep, Anju, Akshay, Aarti and Sonia, thank you for your boundless love and noisy indifference.

Sara, thank you for allowing me to give you a subject to ponder upon during your journey through your teens, and Arjun, thank you for being the jewel in the crown. I hope you too shall imbibe the hobby of birding and nature watching once you get out of the crawling stage.

Many thanks to Dr Kedia for having unwittingly seeded the idea of this book during our endless discussions on mythology.

Thank you, Dr Navneet, Dr Nikhil, Dr Suhel Quadir, Vineet, Col Rajan and Subhashini Ali, in a very special way, for your constant encouragement; and thank you, Thoma, Shahid, Feroz and Gita for being such patient listeners during our long memorable treks along the Ganges.

Akash, thank you for the charcoals that have been brought out so painstakingly – discovering a mountain full of local talent was the best accident to have ever happened.

Purnima, thank you for helping me with the translations. Nobody else could have done it better than you.

Avnish, your skills on the computer are admirable and helped save the day.

Finally, special thanks to the Notion Press team for their unending support in getting to see the book in print.

INTRODUCTION

Over the centuries, man has been deeply fascinated by the ability of his feathered friends to freely soar the skies. He has been inspired by their beauty, power, grace, speed, endurance, intelligence, killing instinct, and above all, their fidelity and infallible spirit. He has held them in awe, and seeing in them the divine and the supernatural, he started relating to them in spiritual and philosophical terms. Birds mystified him and became a part of his folklore, superstitions, allegories, poetry and literature. He domesticated them, spoke to them and even taught them his language. He hunted them and used them for sport and entertainment. Birds became a part of his rituals in both birth and death alike.

In Indian mythology, our seers had the wisdom and insight to understand the character and power of Mother Nature and its impact on mankind. They revered birds and anthropomorphised them. Birds were depicted as the vehicles or mounts of many Indian gods and deities to remind us of the need to overpower our wild instincts and move towards self-realisation. Lord Vishnu rides *Garuda*, Goddess Saraswati is seated on a swan, Murgan, or Kartikeya, rides a peacock, Lord Shani* rides a crow, Kamadeva, the god of love, is seated on a parrot, Goddess Lakshmi rides an owl and so on.

The divine status that birds enjoy in Indian mythology has also built a string of superstitions around them in Indian folklore. Owls, being the mount of Goddess Lakshmi, are considered a good omen by some, while others consider them inauspicious as they believe owls are a manifestation of Alakshmi* – the opposite of Lakshmi. Similarly, crows are believed to be the carriers of food to departed souls, and hence, are fed extensively during the period of Śrāddha*, while the Vedic Indians considered them to be inauspicious and evil. The sighting of an Indian Roller – blue jay – on the day of *Dussehra* is considered auspicious as it is believed to be an incarnation of Lord Shiva, while the peacock has been protected through the ages out of religious sentiments associated with gods such as Lord Krishna.

Birds have enjoyed descriptions in our ancient scriptures and texts: in the *Upanishads, Vedas, Puranas*, *Shastras** and epics such as the *Ramayana* and the *Mahabharata* that date back to many centuries BC. In the *Yajur Samhita**, parrots and mynas were taught to talk and were a source of wisdom and sound advice to humans.

Our Vedic seers had made many accurate observations about bird behaviour, the most specific one amongst them being brood parasitism* prevalent in the cuckoos or the koels. They have appended such observations in their Sanskrit scripts and literature. Doves, eagles, cranes and vultures are some of the many birds that find mention in Indian iconography, mythology, folklore and literature.

Birds also figure prominently in the legendary *Panchatantra** and *Jataka** stories that have been an integral part of Indian folklore for centuries and impart lessons in common wisdom and moral values amongst the younger generation. Importantly, the characteristics that the birds represent in these stories are quite synonymous with the behaviour commonly visible amongst these birds in reality. The influence of birds in Sanskrit and medieval Indian literature is amply visible in Kalidasa's *Meghadūta* and *Abhijñānashākuntala*.

The age-old tradition of feeding birds before meals is practised by followers of different religious faiths even today. Many households maintain feeding trays and birdbaths in their courtyards – a practice considered to be a part of one's religious faith. Feeding pigeons, sparrows, crows and parrots at the main traffic hubs in the heart of a metro city is a common sight even today. Newly married couples are asked to visit and pay obeisance to Sarus cranes, which are known for their fidelity.

The peacock was declared as the national bird because of the stature it enjoys in Indian culture and also because it forms a part of many poetic compositions, motifs and traditional textile designs. The enchanting *Mayura* dance continues to be a part of many cultural performances, and one never tires of marvelling at the dance of the peacock in the wild and when enacted on stage. The *Koel* and *Papiha* too have deeply influenced Indian folklore, and have inspired many writers and poets to pen down numerous classic compositions. The call of a koel announces the onset of spring with the season of sumptuous mangoes around the corner. Birds have strongly influenced Indian folklore and are deeply woven into the tapestry of Indian culture.

BIRD STUDY IN INDIA

While birds have maintained their influence in Indian folklore, ornithology as a subject has remained dormant in India for centuries with no visible effort to develop it on scientific grounds, except for some references in Sanskrit literature. K N Dave, an eminent Sanskrit scholar and ornithologist, in his book *Birds in Sanskrit Literature* made a bold attempt to identify birds and decode bird behaviour based on their mentions in Vedic and Classical Sanskrit literature and in epics such as the Mahabharata and the Ramayana. For example, the Pandavas copied the 'V' flight formation of the cranes in the war against the Kauravas, making a formation of their squadron named *Kranchvu*. This formation has been defined in the *Shukra Niti* (ch. 4, sec.7.297). The *Vanara sena* in the Ramayana had also adopted this formation while attacking Ravana's forces (Ram. VI.69.36-37).

The signs of serious study on birds first became visible during the Mughal period with Emperors Babur and Jahangir* making some accurate observations on bird behaviour and recording them in their memoirs *Tuzk-e-Babri* and *Tuzk-e-Jahangiri*. Jahangir's passion for nature was known far and wide, and he even maintained a personal menagerie. He patronised a school of arts for painting birds and animals and hired the services of the famous artist Ustad Mansur* and honoured him with the title *Nadir-ul-Asr*. Ustad Mansur has to his credit a painting of the nearly extinct Siberian crane that had once visited our Keoladeo Ghana Bird Sanctuary.

With the arrival of the East India Company, scientific ornithology gained significance with many British bureaucrats, tea planters and Civil and British Army officers carrying out studies on regional and provincial birds. Edward Buckley published accounts of 22 Indian birds with descriptions and drawings in the year 1713. Capt. James Franklin studied birds of the Vindhya hills*, while Col. W H Sykes named many Indian birds after Hindu deities such as *Hypsipetes ganeesa* for the Southern Black Bulbul, *Milvus govinda* for the Pariah Kite, and *Hippolais rama* for the Tree Warbler. They carried out studies and collected specimens and published papers on birds of the Deccan region during the period 1831–1832.

Jerdon published two volumes of the classic *Birds of India* during the period 1862–1864. Others who have made significant contributions during this period – termed as the founders of Indian ornithology – were Brian Houghton Hodgson, Edward Blyth and Thomas Caverhill Jerdon, whose writings add great value to the natural history of India. John Gould, a taxidermist, did pioneering work on Himalayan birds through his collection of specimens, and Mrs Gould provided drawings for *A Century of Birds from the Himalayan Mountains,* while N A Vigors did the write-up.

The title of 'The Father' or the 'The Pope' of Indian ornithology goes to Allan Octavian Hume. He was one of the founders of the Indian National Congress. He is credited with that title for having carried out an extensive and systematic recording of the birds of India between years 1870–1885 and collecting over 60,000 specimens across the country. This extensive work of his is now available with the British Museum.

Stray Feathers, a journal of Indian birds, was founded by Hume and edited by him from 1872 to 1888. Further fillip to Indian ornithology came in the year 1898, with the publishing of four volumes of *Fauna of British India* by Oates and Blanford, who consolidated the research on Indian birds for over 27 years. This effort was later reinforced by E C Stuart Baker with the publishing of the second edition of the *Fauna of British India*.

With the founding of the Bombay Natural History Society in 1883, Indian wildlife and ornithology accumulated a wealth of information that is highly relevant till date. The society has contributed enormously towards popularising bird watching and has also laid enormous emphasis on conserving nature. The period also saw the end of the British era, in 1943, with the passing of Dr Claud B Ticehurst and Hugh Whistler, two outstanding contributors to Indian ornithology.

With the emergence of the legendary Dr Salim Ali, Bharat Ratna, in the mid-1930s, Indian ornithology graduated to its next phase – the Golden era. The publishing of the *Handbook of the Birds of India and Pakistan* and the *Book of Indian Birds* gave a new dimension to Indian ornithology. The significance and economic importance of birds and their roles in the ecosystem were addressed, and grave concerns over the depleting flora and fauna and damage to the environment were brought to light during this period. A new generation of Indian ornithologists mushroomed over the Indian scene. With the advent of revolutionary printing and photography technologies, many field guides by authors such as Richard Grimmett, Carol and Tim Inskipp, Krys Kazmierczak and Bikram Grewal flooded bookshelves, while *Birds of India* and *Birds, Beyond Watching* by Abdul Jamil Urfi added to the literary chest of Indian ornithology. The lesser-known Hindi books *Shikar ke Pakshi* and *Bharat ke Pakshi* by Suresh Singh and Rajeswarprasad Narain Singh added flavour to bird watching – a hobby that had by then became a popular pastime.

The damage to the environment by the indiscriminate use of pesticides and drugs and the loss of habitats has seen the near extinction of vultures and a sharp decline in the abundance of sparrows and many other birds in the Indian sky. What needs to be seen in the days to come is whether the golden technologies are outpaced by the extinction of birds, or whether there are some birds still left for technology to preserve.

PART I

MYTHICAL BIRDS

GARUDA

Sanskrit: Garuda, Chirada, Gaganeshvara, Kamayusha, Kashyapi, Khageshvara, Nagantaka, Sitanana, Sudhahara, Suparna, Syena, Tarkshya, Tarswin, Vainateya, Vishnuratha

Common names: Vainetey, Nagari, Nagbhishan, Jitantak, Vishari, Ajit, Vishwaroopi, Garutmaan, Khagshreshtha, Kashyapnandan

Garuda is a large Hindu mythical bird with a golden-coloured human body. It has an eagle's head and beak with four arms and red wings. In the Mahabharata, it is revered for its great violent force and speed. It is highly enlightened, and is an embodiment of strong virtues. The king of all birds of prey, Garuda is the divine vehicle of Vishnu*. Born to his father Kashyapa* and mother Vinata*, he is the brother of another mythical bird Aruna*. He is also the husband of Rudra and Sukeerthi. Garuda is also the Hindu name for the constellation *Aquila*.

HOW GARUDA BECAME VISHNU'S MOUNT

As the legend goes, Garuda had taken it upon himself to rescue his mother Vinata from the bondage of his stepmother Kadru – a *Nagini** and the mother of all serpents. In exchange for his mother's freedom, the serpents demanded that Garuda fetch them *amrita** – the elixir of life – from the heavens, where the gods were zealously guarding it. The chamber where the amrita was stored was guarded by two poisonous serpents, and it had a huge fire encircling it. Garuda defeated the gods and then extinguished the fire with his mouth filled with water from many rivers. He killed the snakes and carried the amrita in his beak without swallowing it.

On his way back, Garuda met Vishnu who offered him the gift of immortality in return for the amrita. As a reward for not consuming the amrita, Vishnu promised to make Garuda his mount.

HOW GARUDA AVENGED THE TREATMENT METED BY THE SERPENTS TO HIS MOTHER

Indra* conspired with Garuda to maliciously regain the possession of the amrita and return it to the gods in heaven once it was delivered as promised to the serpents. Thus, after delivering the amrita to the serpents, Garuda urged the serpents to perform their rituals before consuming it. As they hurried off to perform the rituals, Indra swooped up the amrita and decamped with it. In return, Indra offered the serpents to Garuda as his food, thus helping Garuda avenge the treatment meted out by the serpents to his mother.

From that day onwards, Garuda became the trusted mount of Vishnu and the everlasting enemy of the serpents.

GARUDA: MYTHS AND STORIES

In the Ramayana*, Garuda – the archenemy of the serpents and Vishnu's mount – was sent at the behest of Hanuman* to rescue Rama* and Laxmana* after Indrajit, the son of Ravana*, tied them with the *Nagpashastra* – a biological weapon made of a million poisonous serpents.

When returning from the heavens with the amrita in his beak, Garuda had perched on a *kadamba* tree and wiped his beak against its branch. A drop of amrita fell on the branch at that time, and thus immortalised the kadamba tree.

Legend has it that Mayura, the son of Garuda, was created from the feathers of Garuda. The images of Mayura depict the majestic bird killing a serpent.

Garuda is amongst the beings appointed by Indra, and he also guards Mount Sumeru and the heavens from the onslaught of the *asuras**.

The Garudas are the archenemies of the Nagas*, the serpents, whom they hunt and seize by their heads. The Nagas learnt that by swallowing large stones, they would become too heavy to be carried by the Garudas, thus killing them from exhaustion. This secret was shared with Garuda by an ascetic Karambiya, who taught Garuda how to seize a Naga by the tail and force him to vomit out the stone. Worshipping Garuda is believed to remove the effects of poisons from one's body.

Krishna* and Satyabhama* are known to have ridden on Garuda to kill Narakasura*.

On another occasion, Lord Hari is believed to have ridden on Garuda to save a devotee elephant Gajendra*.

Garuda is said to have taken 500 years to hatch from an egg. His glowing face appeared as a raging inferno and made the people think that he was Agni* himself. The flapping of his wings created cyclonic storms that darkened the sky and blew down houses. Frightened, the gods begged Garuda for mercy. Having paid heed to their pleas, Garuda reduced himself in size and energy.

An independent Upanishad*, a Hindu scripture, is devoted to Garuda – the *Garuda Purana*.

GARUDA AS A SYMBOL

With Vishnu as their protector, the Garuda race is known to be of great might and without compassion, and they have been adopted as symbols both in ancient and modern India, chiefly as military symbols.

In the Mahabharata, Drona* used a military formation, *Garuda Vyuha,* that was in the shape of an eagle and was named after Garuda. In this formation, Bhishma was at its beak, while Drona and Kritavarna were at the eyes; Kripa and Ashwathama were at the head positions, while Duryodhana and his brothers formed the main body of the Garuda.

Even Lord Krishna carried the image of Garuda on his banner.

The elite bodyguards of the medieval Hoysala kings – in Karnataka, India – were named Garudas because they served the king in the way Garuda served Vishnu.

The Brigade of the Guards – an Infantry Battalion of the Indian Army – has adopted Garuda as its insignia.

The Garud Commando force is a Special Forces Unit of the Indian Air Force, specialising in operations carried deep behind enemy lines.

GARUDA: IN ORNITHOLOGY

As per the Mahabharata, all birds of prey descended from Garuda. Their names in Sanskrit and Hindi denote the physical traits and the mythological aspects of different birds, though it may not always be easy to identify or link a particular bird with its mythical counterpart.

The names Garuda, *Tarkshya* and *Vainateya* are synonymous with *Suparna**, a name specific to the Himalayan Golden Eagle. It is also known as *Mahavir,* not only for its mythological exploits but also for being courageous and bold by nature. One of the faces of the *Panchamukha* (five-faced) *Hanuman** – pointing in the western direction – is that of Mahavira Garuda.

The name Suparna is also synonymous in the *Rig Veda** for the Seven Eagles (Genus Aquilas), i.e., Himalayan Golden Eagle, Imperial Eagle, Steppe Eagle, Indian Tawny Eagle, Greater Spotted Eagle, Smaller Spotted Eagle and Lammergeier. It also implies that Garuda had imbibed the traits of all the aforesaid eagles.

ARUNA

Sanskrit: Aruna

A mythical bird in Hindu mythology, *Aruna* is a manifestation of the rising Sun and is Surya's* charioteer. He is the son of sage Kashyap and Vinata, brother of Garuda, and the father of Jatayu and *Sampati**. Described as birds, Garuda and Aruna were given the authority by their father Kashyap to rule over the birds.

HOW ARUNA GOT THE GLOW OF THE RISING SUN

As the legend goes, Aruna and Garuda were born from the same clutch of eggs. Their mother Vinata had been given a boon that the sons born to her would be strong and powerful if she allowed the eggs to hatch on their own. However, impatience got the better of her and she broke one of the eggs, and from it – with a flash, lightning and thunder – emerged the legendry Aruna, as radiant as the rising Sun.

ARUNA: IN ORNITHOLOGY

Mythical Aruna is the father of Jatayu and Sampati. All three are interrelated and belong to the family of vultures. Their names denote characteristics and traits attributed to different vultures. Aruna is the Black or King Vulture (*Sarcogyps calvus*) with red underparts synonymous with the colour of the Sun. Sampati, of gregarious habits, is the Indian Griffon Vulture (*Gyps fulvus*) and Jatayu, the bearded one, is none other than the Bearded Vulture (*Gypaetus barbatus*) or the Lammergeier.

JATAYU

Sanskrit: Jatayu

Jatayu, a mythical bird, is the King of Vultures. He is the son of Aruna – Surya's Charioteer – and Syeni – the daughter of Daksha*. He is the younger half-brother of Sampati, nephew of Garuda and a friend of King Dasharatha*.

HOW JATAYU IS SAVED BY SAMPATI FROM BEING SEARED BY THE SUN

Jatayu and Sampati were brothers who spent a lot of time playing and competing with each other. One day, they decided to jointly scale the skies in competition and see who could fly higher. They started soaring high into the skies and went too close to the

Sun. Suddenly, Jatayu felt the Sun's rays were too hot to bear. Seeing his brother in distress, Sampati rushed to Jatayu's rescue by spreading his wings to prevent the Sun's rays from hurting him. In the process, Sampati burnt both his wings and went crashing down to earth. After that, Sampati could never fly or take to the skies again and was separated from Jatayu.

HOW JATAYU CONFRONTED RAVANA AND ATTEMPTED TO RESCUE SITA

Jatayu noticed Ravana while he was abducting Sita* in an *Uddan khatola**. He put up a valiant fight with Ravana in an attempt to rescue Sita. In the fight that ensued, Ravana mortally wounded Jatayu and cut off his wings. Jatayu held on to his life and waited for Rama and Laxmana to share the whereabouts of Sita with them. Meanwhile, Rama and Laxmana encountered Jatayu by chance while searching for Sita. They learnt that Jatayu had been an old friend of their father, Dasharatha. When they told him about their search for Sita, Jatayu narrated about his fight with Ravana and showed them the direction in which Ravana had taken Sita.

HOW JATAYU ATTAINED MOKSHA

After sensing that injured Jatayu's end had come, Rama, who was Vishnu's incarnation, decided to grant *moksha** to him. Rama hit an arrow on the ground, and called all the seven rivers, *Teertha,* to the spot. All the rivers responded except for *Gaya Teertha,* which was then forced by Rama to come to the spot. Jatayu was given the water of all the seven rivers and attained moksha and was sent to the heavens. The six rivers that responded to Rama's call fell into one single pond, while *Gaya Teertha* fell a few feet away as a punishment and joined the other six invisibly. The place is known as Taaked in Nasik District, and a fair is held there on the day of *Mahashivratri**. In another version, the location where Jatayu fights Ravana is a place called Chadayamangalam. It is a village in Kollam District in the state of Kerala. Its name was derived from the name Jatayumangalam, where a huge rock is named after Jatayu, and it is a place of attraction for tourists.

In Tamil Nadu*, approximately 27 km from Chidambaram*, is a place called Vaitheeswaran Koil. There exists a temple which has a pond dedicated to Jatayu and also has his metal image installed in its precincts.

JATAYU: IN ORNITHOLOGY

Jatayu – also known as *Vat* in Sanskrit – has beardlike aerial-roots or the *Jatals* of the Indian Fig tree *(Ficus benghalensis)* or the banyan tree *(Bargadh*)*. He is referred to as the *Mahagidh* in the Ramayana. He is described as a bird that has a goatee or tufts of long black bristle-like hair below its chin with red eyes, white breasts and a large body that aptly fits the description of the Bearded Vulture or the Lammergeier *(Gypaetus barbatus)*.

SAMPATI

Sanskrit: Sampati

Sampati is one of Aruna's two sons and the brother of Jatayu. He was instrumental in ultimately leading Hanuman to Ravana's palace where Sita was held captive. *Gridhraj Parvat* – situated in Satna District in Madhya Pradesh – is believed to be the birthplace of Sampati.

HOW SAMPATI LOST HIS WINGS

As the story goes, during their childhood, Sampati and Jatayu were competing as to who could fly higher and touch the Sun. As they flew closer to the Sun, Jatayu felt the intense heat of the Sun's flames and asked Sampati to provide shelter and rescue him. Sampati spread his large wings above Jatayu in the manner that vultures do to shield their chicks from the Sun's heat. The Sun's flames were so intense that they burnt Sampati's wings, and he came crashing down to earth. Because of the fall, Sampati remained unconscious for more than three days. On regaining consciousness, Sampati realised that he had lost his wings and could not fly again, and hence, he could not go in search of his brother Jatayu. In the bargain, Jatayu too lost complete contact with Sampati and gave him up for dead.

HOW SAMPATI HELPED END THE SEARCH FOR SITA

As Lord Rama moved through the forests searching for Sita, search parties were sent in different directions to look for her.

One such party – led by Hanuman, Angada*, and Jambuvana* – were sent down South. Tired and disappointed, they came to the end of the land and found a large expanse of sea. With no place to go, they stopped to rest. That's when they heard the deep hoarse voice of Sampati, who was a griffon of gregarious habits and was extremely delighted to have a fresh consignment of live food served to him at his doorstep.

Hanuman, Angada and Jambuvana begged for mercy and pleaded with Sampati that they be allowed to complete their search for Sita first and then return and offer themselves for sacrifice. With Sampati in no mood to relent, Jambuvana compared the moral values of the inconsiderate Sampati with that of Jatayu who had laid down his life protecting Sita. On hearing about his brother Jatayu, Sampati, with tears rolling down from his eyes, mourned the demise of his long-lost brother Jatayu and begged Jambuvana to tell him more about Jatayu. Jambuvana described at length about the heroic fight Jatayu had put up to prevent Sita's abduction.

Sampati, who was the nephew of Garuda, was blessed with eyesight extraordinaire, just like how all vultures are. He had seen Sita's abduction by Ravana. He vowed to avenge Jatayu's death and offered to lead Hanuman, Angada and Jambuvana to Lanka and to Ravana's palace where Sita was held captive.

SAMPATI: IN ORNITHOLOGY

Because of his gregarious habits, Sampati is likened to the Indian Griffon Vulture (*Gypus fulvus*).

MAYURA

Hindi: Mor, Manjur, Mayura

Sanskrit: Kaalkanth, Neelkanth, Neelang, Bahulgreev, Mahamayur, Rajsaras, Shitikanth, Sarpari, Sarang

Mayura*, meaning peacock, is highly revered and respected in Hindu, Islamic and Buddhist mythologies and has a pivotal place in Indian art and folklore. It symbolises pride, beauty, arrogance, fertility, dignity, immortality and wisdom in different cultures. It is the progeny of the mythical bird Garuda. It is believed that Mayura was created from Garuda's feathers.

In Hindu mythology, the mayura is the mount of many Indian gods and goddesses. In Islam, Allah created the peacock and placed it atop the *Sajaratul Yaakin** tree. In Buddhism, it symbolises wisdom. It was because of the mayura's inviolable status and the niche that it had created for itself in Indian folklore and the cultural fabric that it was adopted as India's national bird.

HOW THE MAYURA IS DEPICTED AS THE MOUNT OF HINDU DEITIES

As the divine vehicle of different Hindu deities, the mayura represents multifarious attributes, both positive and negative, when associated with each deity separately.

As the mount of Kartikeya* or Murugan* – the god of war – it is swift and beautiful and represents splendour. As the legend goes, the mayura's ability to destroy snakes is attributed to its relationship with Kartikeya.

When seated beside Goddess Saraswati*, the mayura represents arrogance and pride. In another interpretation, it is the devourer of snakes with the alchemical ability to metamorphose the serpent's poison into the peacock's iridescent plumage, ostensibly meaning that self-realisation leads to enlightenment. The graceful peacock represents wisdom as Saraswati is the controller of the pursuit of all performing arts. The peacock beside Saraswati also signifies control over pride, fear and indecision and urges one not to be fickle-minded if true knowledge is to be acquired. It also insists that one be conscious and wise of the eternal truth.

In some depictions, there is a serpent coiled around the peacock, such as at the famous Kapaleeshwarar Temple in

Chennai. The coiled serpent around the peacock symbolises man's ego. The peacock keeps the serpent under its control but does not kill it, thereby signifying tolerance.

The mayura signifies fertility when depicted and worn as an armband by Goddess Lakshmi, the consort of Lord Vishnu.

In Orissa, the Gotipua folk dance is associated with Lord Krishna, where the mayura signifies splendour and majesty. Lord Krishna, who is also the irresistible divine suitor, is shown in the company of peacocks. Its feathers have always adorned Lord Krishna's head. It was perhaps this attribute, which leads to the recommendation in the *Kama Sutra* that men may wear a peacock's bone which is embedded in gold and tied to the right hand to improve their looks. According to folklore, the mayura learnt how to dance after witnessing Lord Krishna performing the *Raas Leela** with the *gopis**.

The mayura's friendship with Lord Krishna is legendary, such that Krishna is also known as *Mormukatadhari*. Legend has it that the King of Peacocks offered his feathers to Krishna as '*Gurudakshina*' in return for his having consented to dance with them. So as not to displease his devotees, Krishna adorned them in his headgear for all time to come.

Once, Shiva* was imparting lessons to Parvati* when she got distracted by a beautiful peacock. This annoyed Shiva and he cursed Parvati to take birth as a peahen. He promised that he would rejoin her only after she worshipped him. To free herself from the curse, Parvati worshipped Shiva in the form of a peacock at a place called Mylapore in Chennai, wherein stands the famous Kapaleeshwarar Temple.

As the mount of Kama, the god of love, the peacock represents desire.

HOW THE MAYURA GOT ITS COLOURFUL FEATHERS

Indra, the god of the heavens, was once involved in a duel with Ravana who had invaded the heavens and forced Indra to flee. The mayura – then a bird with ordinary brown plumage – was witnessing the battle. It took pity on Indra and opened its feathers, forming a screen between Ravana and Indra, thus helping Indra to hide behind its feathers. Indra was deeply touched by this gesture and blessed the mayura with its beautiful green and blue feathers. As it was blessed by the rain god, Indra, the mayura dances with the onset of the *varsha ritu**, thus welcoming the rains and the rain god, Indra. It is believed that whenever Indra transforms himself into an animal, he takes the form of the mayura. Indra also blessed the mayura to be fearless of the serpents.

HOW THE MAYURA BECAME THE MOUNT OF KARTIKEYA

As the myth goes, the demon Surapadman was locked in a battle with Kartikeya and took shelter under the deep ocean as a mango tree. Kartikeya, on spotting the demon, hurled a spear at him, splitting the mango tree into two. From one half emerged the peacock, while a rooster emerged from the other. Kartikeya took the peacock as his mount and the rooster as the symbol of his flag.

HOW ALLAH CREATED THE PEACOCK

The legend has it that the peacock was created by Allah – from the light of Muhammad – and was placed on the *Sajaratul Yaakin* tree. Perched on the tree, the peacock prayed to Allah for seventy thousand years using rosary beads. Deeply touched by the peacock's devotion, Allah placed a mirror of shame in front of him. So enamoured was the peacock by its beauty that he prostrated five times before Allah to thank him, and this led to the tradition of the Muslims praying to Allah five times a day.

THE MAYURA IN INDIAN POETRY, LITERATURE AND FOLK SONGS

The mayura has been a great source of inspiration for Indian poets through the ages. In Kalidasa's *Shakuntala,* Dushyanta* refuses to shoot the dancing mayura while on a hunt as it reminds him of how Shakuntala's* hair, adorned with different flowers, got disarrayed during their lovemaking. In *Meghdootam*, Kalidasa* has used the peacock to depict sorrow, pain and anguish arising out of separation. In the Ramayana, Valmiki* has made frequent references to the calls of peacocks while describing the forests through which Rama passes.

Indian classical and folklore music is rich with the mayura motif. In the *varsha rituragas,* a mayura's call depicts both the lover's celebration of union – *samyog* – and pain on separation – *viyog rasa.* Kumar Gandharva's* composition *'Brindhavan, Kyon Na Bhaye Hum Mor'* is a musical masterpiece.

The peacock frequently appears in Rajasthani, Bhojpuri*, Braj* and Avadhi* folk songs. It is portrayed as an ideal lover in contradiction to its polygamous nature.

THE MUGHAL OF THE BIRD KINGDOM

Though a peacock is polygamous and maintains a modest harem of four to five peahens, its failure to satisfy the nymphets has earned it the title of the 'Grand Mughal of the Bird Kingdom.' Little wonder then that it was treated indifferently and with considerable disrespect by the maids.

PEACOCK FEATHERS AND THEIR USES

In Indian culture, peacock feathers form an emblem of pride and rank. They are used for decoration, medicine and witchcraft, and they are in great demand within and outside the country. The collection of peacock feathers is a cause of great concern to conservationists as it leads to heavy poaching of the bird despite the protection accorded to it under the law.

Different concoctions are prepared from peacock feathers and prescribed by quacks and Ayurvedic physicians in Kerala and Tamil Nadu. In Punjab, it is used along with tobacco as an antidote for snakebites. In witchcraft, tied feather strings are used for healing of wounds, fever and curing diseases; it is also used as an antidote for vomiting and snakebite, as protective medicine and for warding off demons.

Peacock feathers are considered sacred; they are an essential part of temple rituals and festivals in Kerala. In Gujarat, peacock feathers have special significance for the *Rabaris*; they form a part of the rituals of the *Madh* ceremony which is meant for invoking the goddesses.

Buddhists use it for sprinkling water on the altar. Finding a peacock feather is considered auspicious by some, who believe it to be equivalent to getting Lord Vishnu's *darshan**.

In Jainism, it is customary for monks to carry a broom made of fallen peacock feathers and clean the floors with it before sleeping so as not to hurt the lowly insects.

In another myth, the peacock and the peahen do not mate physically. The peahen instead gets pregnant by drinking the tears from the peacock's eyes while it is dancing; hence peacocks are considered pure like Lord Krishna and are found worthy of having their feather in Krishna's crown.

PEACOCK DANCE AND ITS SIGNIFICANCE

With the onset of the monsoon, the peacock's dance mesmerises one and all, and many interpretations exist about its true purpose.

Some see the awesome performance as one to invoke jealousies amongst competitors as well as an amorous advance towards the peahens. The instinct to display not only exists amongst the males but also amongst the females and the chicks, thus mystifying the biological purpose of the dance. In one particular instance, a peacock was seen indulging in this display before a tortoise. In another instance, an intruding male peacock was seen being violently chased away by a dancing male who was performing before its harem of female peahens.

While the debate continues, the peacock's dance continues to captivate one and all through the ages, be it poets, writers or performers. In fact, Birju Maharaj reflects upon the arrogance, pride and grace of a peacock in his performance in the *Kathak* style of Indian dance. Tribes across the country have the peacock dance as a primary theme in their respective folk dances. The adoption of the peacock dance by the theatre and displays during festivals is a common occurrence.

PEACOCK WORSHIP

In India, the peacock is considered auspicious. It is widely worshipped in the country, mainly in the South where the *Pavolatry Cult** is prevalent amongst the Dravidians* who propitiate it as Mother Earth. It is also deified by the Tamilians as Kartikeya or Murugan and is worshipped during the festival of *Pongal**. In Northern India, peacock feathers have all along adorned Lord Krishna's headgear. The peacock is used as a symbol by many clans in Southern India, by the Bhils* of Central India, by the Jats in Northern India and by the Guptas who had the peacock as their royal bird. The Maurya Dynasty had the origins of its name from the term mayura. Peacock figures can also be seen on the pottery of the Indus Valley and the Harappan eras.

MAYURA: MYTHS AND LEGENDS

In Indian folklore, the mayura has the intuitive powers of predicting rains, and its call and dance announces the arrival of the monsoons.

There are many variations about how the peacock got its ugly feet. According to a Kangra* legend, the myna, which had ugly feet, went out to the peacock and borrowed his beautiful dancing feet to attend a wedding, promising to return the same after the event was over. The myna, however, cheated the peacock and refused to return the same. The peacock, to date, laments for having trusted the myna.

In another variation, the peacock and the myna had a dancing match when the peacock still had its pretty feet. The myna asked the peacock to lend him the same so that the peacock could see him dance. The myna, instead of returning the feet, decamped and never came back. It is believed that the peacock weeps every time he sees his feet and regrets the foolish decision.

Many interpret this as a symbolic reminder of not brooding over one's shortcomings and, instead, rejoicing over one's strengths.

The peacock is considered as a symbol of an ideal lover, and its figure is depicted on the walls and floors of the *Kohbar* or marriage booths in many Indian weddings.

In Christianity, there is a belief that the peacock's flesh is incorruptible, and hence, it symbolises Christ's resurrection and promises immortality.

THE MAYURA IN MOTIFS

The mayura has been used extensively as a motif through the ages and across the country. Kings and dynasties used it on their flagstaffs and artists used it as a theme on their stone, bronze and terracotta sculptures and paintings. Mayura designs have been exploited commercially – in advertisements and in traditional textile prints; on greeting cards, hoardings, trucks, temple lamps and coins and stamps; as weaves and patterns of the famous *Kantha* and *Banarsi* sarees and as trademarks and decorations. Folk artists and women in villages often use it on their house walls.

AS INDIA'S NATIONAL BIRD

The peacock was chosen as India's national bird way back in 1963 because of its rich cultural, religious and legendary involvement in Indian traditions, myths and folklore. The peacock is widely distributed throughout the country and is easily recognisable by the common man; it is not confused with the emblem of any other nation. The bird is protected under Sec 51, 1-A of the Wild Life (Protection) Act, 1972 and killing it is strictly prohibited. The export of peacock tail feathers and articles and handicrafts made from them are banned under the Convention on International Trade in Endangered Species and the export-import policy of India.

PEACOCK THRONE (MAYURASAN OR TAKHT-E-TAVUS)

The peacock has been symbolic of the pleasures of the courts in Islamic culture. It is commonly depicted in Mughal miniatures where peacocks are seen roaming in the gardens and palaces of the Islamic noblemen. It was the peacock's beauty, splendour and grace that triggered the imagination of the Mughal ruler Shah Jahan* to visualise the fabulous Peacock Throne. It took his chief goldsmith Bibadal Khan seven years, the famous diamond *Koh-i-noor*, 230 kgs of rubies, garnets, pearls and 1150 kgs of pure gold to bring to life the fabulous Peacock Throne. The throne had figures of two standing peacocks which were thickly inset with gems, and between them, a tree with a foliage of rubies, diamonds and pearls. Nader Shah of Persia invaded the Mughal Empire in 1739 and took with him the priceless Peacock Throne as war booty. After Nader Shah's assassination in 1747, the throne was stolen and dismantled and lost for posterity. Some believe it was lost in the Indian Ocean while being transported by the British to England in June 1782 aboard the ill-fated ship *Grosvenor*. However, the gracefulness of the peacocks embedded in the throne continues to awe us even today.

MAYURA: IN ORNITHOLOGY

One of the most gorgeous-looking birds on the Indian subcontinent, the peacock (*Pavo cristatus*) belongs to the order *Gallinaceous* and the family *Phasianidae*. The polygamous male moves with his harem of 4–5 females. It has an iridescent blue neck and breast and an ornamental glossy green elongated tail — the upper tail coverts that are best displayed during the elaborate courtship dance. Both male and the female carry a crest. The peahen (female) lacks the ornamental train and is mottled brown and metallic green on the lower neck.

Generally shy and extremely alert, the bird is distributed throughout the Indian Union up to 1800m in the Himalayas. It feeds on lizards, snakes, insects, vegetable shoots and grains, and it takes to flight reluctantly. It breeds during January to October and nests on the ground, with a shallow scrape lined with twigs and leaves.

HAMSA

Hindi: Hans, Rajhans

Sanskrit: Pakhans, Mahahans

Hamsa or the *Raj Hansa,* the swan, is highly revered in Hinduism and enjoys a mythical status in Hindu mythology. It is the *Hamsa–Vahini* or the carrier bird of Saraswati – the goddess of learning and eloquence – and Brahma* – the creator of the Universe and the consort of Saraswati.

The hamsa is considered a symbol of knowledge and wisdom. It represents the ideals of spiritual purity and goodness. It is likened to *Paramhansa* – the supreme soul or the saintly one – who has the virtue of remaining detached from the world. In another interpretation, the long serpentine neck of the hamsa embodies the union between two archenemies, or the two opposites, i.e., Garuda and Naga, thus symbolising the highest level of wisdom.

In the Upanishads, the hamsa is described as the 'King of Birds.' It feeds on pearls, and it has the *Neera –Ksheera viveka,* or the mythical power to separate milk from water, thus symbolising its capacity to differentiate between knowledge and ignorance, good and evil, and relevant from irrelevant. The changing value systems in today's era have made lyricists represent the purity of the hamsa in the couplet *'Ram Chandra keh gaye siya se, aisa kalyug aayega, hans khayega dana tinka, kauwah roti khayega.'* (Lord Rama tells Sita that in the coming era, swans shall eat straws while the crows shall feast on bread.)

It is conjectured that the hamsa resides in *devlok** or the gods' abode in present-day Lake Manasarovar near *Kailash Parbat* beyond the Himalayas.

THE HAMSA AS A MESSENGER OF LOVERS

The hamsa, besides its mythical status, famously plays the role of a messenger between lovers in Hindu mythology.

Poet Vedanta Desika – in his famous love poem *Hamsa-Sandesha* – describes how Lord Rama uses the hamsa as a messenger to carry his message to Sita while Ravana held her captive. In the poem, Rama also explains to the hamsa the route it should follow to reach Sita and the places of pilgrimage where he needs to stop over en route.

In the love story of *Nala–Damayanti* in the Mahabharata, Nala, the virtuous King of Nishadha, falls in love and dreams of marrying Damayanti*, the Princess of Vidharbha* and the most beautiful woman on earth. One day, Nala captures a hamsa and releases it only after it agrees to plead Nala's cause before Damayanti. The hamsa reaches the palace of Damayanti and allows itself to be captured by her. It speaks in praise of Nala's virtues. Damayanti – on hearing Nala's praises from the hamsa – falls in love with him and dreams of marrying him. The swan returns to Nala and asks him to reach for Damayanti's *swayamwara* * where Damayanti chooses him as her husband.

In *Brihatkathāmanjari* *, Kshemendra relates how Dharmsen and his wife had intently watched a pair of flying swans before their death and were reborn as a pair of raj hamsas.

Damayanti and the swan-messenger
Painting by Raja Ravi Varma

THE HAMSA IN THE RAMAYANA

According to a story in the Ramayana, Varuna – the god of the sky, water and the oceans – avoided confrontation with Ravana by transforming himself into a hamsa. Varuna was so pleased with the form of the hamsa that he granted it the boon of becoming completely white.

THE HAMSA IN THE MAHABHARATA (THE STORY OF DHRITARASHTRA'S BLINDNESS)

Mourning the death of his hundred sons, the Kauravas*, Dhritarashtra* questioned Lord Krishna about the reason for his blindness and the cause for him losing his right to ascend the throne. Lord Krishna asked him to meditate to get the answer to his question. After deep meditation, Dhritarashtra realised that he was a victim of his actions during his previous birth when, as a tyrant king, he had senselessly derived pleasure at blinding a swan and killing its chicks. Hence, during his rebirth as King Dhritarashtra, he was born blind and lost his hundred sons in war.

THE HAMSA IN SANSKRIT LITERATURE

The hamsa has been described as *Devpakshin* or *Hansa-satmaha* – the best of their kind. In old Sanskrit literature, Hamsa is likened to the full moon in a clear blue and starry sky on a lake studded with lilies.

The hamsa is also compared to *Paramhamsa* or a spiritually elevated man. As per etymology and in philosophical terms, 'Param' is a prefix to 'Parameshwara' or the supreme god and 'Hamsa' for the Swan is noted for discipline, grace and beauty. Thus hamsa is symbolic to Paramhamsa or the highest standard of personal grace and ethical behaviour for an honourable person.

THE HAMSA IN THE GURU GRANTH SAHIB

The *Guru Granth Sahib*, the holy book of the Sikhs, has many references in praise of the hamsa's spiritual qualities. In the *Gurbani**, it says that a crane does not become a hamsa in their company, and the hamsa too does not get into an alliance with the crane. The hamsa feeds on pearls, while the crane feeds on frogs and the crane flies away so that its secret does not get exposed. It means that one would get only what the Guru wills for one.

In another verse, it says that the Guru is like an ocean of pearls and the Sikhs, like the swans, gather only if the Guru wills so, and the oceans shall remain full of pearls even if the swan eats them. The Guru wills that the ocean and the swan should not separate. It means that a Sikh shall come to the Guru only when the Guru wills it, and such a *Gursikh** ferries across the world ocean and saves his family and the whole world.

THE HAMSA IN SYMBOLOGY

The hamsa is one of the many sacred Hindu didactic* icons from the Vedic age and is considered to be an important and noble symbol that represents wisdom and beauty. The symbol has become a popular motif in Indian folk art and is commonly used in Kanchipuram saris, textiles, jewellery and Kashmiri carpets.

HAMSA: IN ORNITHOLOGY

Swans, or Raj Hansa, are white, graceful, wise and solitary birds with long necks. They are monogamous and remain in pairs. They are known for their fidelity. They stay with their partners even when one of them is injured and refuse to move even if at risk, prompting lyricists to represent the trait in a melancholic manner in the famous Hindi song: *"Do hanson ka jora bichar gayo re, gajab hayo ram julum hayo re."* They make excellent parents. The mother carries her young ones on her back when they need to rest and also protects them aggressively. They fly in 'V' formations.

Swans are amongst the largest of the flying birds with a wingspan of 10 feet. They reach a length of over 1.5 m and weigh over 15 kgs. They belong to the duck family *Anatidae*. According to Salim Ali, the famous Indian ornithologist, three different types of swans are spotted in India:

1. Bewick's Swan (*Cygnus bewickii*), which is the Eurasian form that migrates from Arctic Russia to western Europe and eastern Asia

2. Whooper Swan (*Cygnus Cygnus*), which breeds in Iceland and Subarctic Europe and Asia and migrates to temperate Europe and Asia in winter

3. Mute Swan (*Cygnus olor*), which is a Eurasian species that occurs across Europe and migrates to southern Russia and China

A group of Indian ornithologists, however, contests that the Raj Hansa mentioned in the Vedas* is the Bar-headed goose or the Greylag goose and not the swan, as swans are not commonly spotted in India. However, in the Vedas, swans are said to reside on Lake Manasarovar.

In Chitrakathi paintings from Maharashtra, the hamsa appears as a crane or a stork, and in modern art, it appears as a goose, a crane or a swan. Scholars state that since the goose is more native to the Indian subcontinent than a swan, the goose is more likely to be the hamsa than a swan. But since the swan is any day more elegant than the goose, the swan remains Saraswati's sacred bird as per popular belief.

In Maharashtra, the crane or stork is depicted as Saraswati's vahana* in the Chitrakathi paintings, thus creating a confusion whether the hamsa was a swan, a crane or a stork. Since the crane's ability to stand on one leg in water while hunting for fish is an embodiment of concentration, it becomes worthy of being associated with Saraswati.

GANDABERUNDA AND SHARABAH

Gandaberunda is a mythical two-headed bird in Hindu mythology. It is believed to have incredible strength and magical powers. It is double-headed with eagle-like features and long peacock-like tail feathers. It is depicted as carrying four elephants – two in its beaks and two in its claws. It is the most fearsome and destructive personification of Narasimha or Lord Vishnu, while Sharabah is an incarnation of Lord Shiva in the form of a mythical beast that was part lion and part bird with blazing wings representing Goddesses Kali and Durga. After Hiranyakashyap* was killed by Narasimha, it was Sharabah that subdued Gandaberunda.

Gandaberunda (a manifestation of Narasimha) as a roof sculpture in Rameshwara temple

Sharabah

Shiva depicted as a two-headed creature,
holding Narasimha in his claws

After having destroyed the demon Hiranyakashyap, Narasimha continued to remain in rage and failed to shelve its beastly form of half-man and half-lion. The destructive powers of Narasimha had the demigods worried, who went pleading to Lord Shiva asking him to intervene and pacify Narasimha. Shiva – who knew Lord Vishnu's power – was aware of the possible consequences of remaining a mute witness to the happenings. He incarnated himself as Sharabah and took Narasimha into an embrace in an attempt to pacify him. Narasimha – who was in a fit of rage – was in no mood to relent, and the two were engaged in combat that lasted for eighteen days before Sharabah was able to force Narsimha* into submission. Later, according to belief, both Sharabah (Shiva) and Narasimha (Vishnu) shed their respective beastly manifestations and transformed back into their usual form. Calm was thus restored in the three worlds.

In another version, Gandaberunda was torn apart by Sharabah after Narasimha submitted to him, while Sharabah was devoured by Goddess Durga.

Gandaberunda has its origins from the Kannada language in Karnataka and is on the Coat of Arms of the Wodeyars – the erstwhile rulers of Karnataka.

GANDABERUNDA AND SHARABAH: IN ORNITHOLOGY

Considering the magical powers and the insurmountable strength of Gandaberunda, one can only infer that such strength and power could only be drawn from the Aquila class of eagles. The depiction of Gandaberunda with twin eagle heads and a single body only enhances its mythical powers that it imbibes from the powerful Aquila eagles with a sense of exaggeration. The powerful claws that show Gandaberunda carrying elephants are similar to the claws of the Aquila class of eagles that are known to be capable of carrying animals of the size of goats.

Since Sharabah was to be more powerful than Gandaberunda so as to be able to subdue him, it is depicted with the double-headed, eagle-like features of Gandaberunda and additionally with the beastly features of two lions, thus making it stronger than Gandaberunda.

PART II

COMMON BIRDS

CHAKOR

Sanskrit: Chakor

Chukar or Chakor (*Alectoris chukar*) is a legendary Indian hill bird that belongs to the family of partridges and prominently appears in regional Indian folklore, folk songs, Sanskrit, Hindi and other regional literature. It is symbolic of intense and everlasting love, and it derives its name from the Sanskrit word chakor, which has been retained in the English language without dilution.

CHAKOR: MYTHS AND STORIES

It is believed that the chakor is passionately devoted to the moon and hence constantly gazes at it, shedding tears while longing for its beloved. In another mythological belief, the chakor thrives on moonlight for its food, with moonlight being its nectar or amrita. Some believe that as the moon travels through the night sky, the chakor too keeps moving its neck, never to take its eyes off the moon.

Legend also has it that the chakor feeds on burning charcoal and the burning charcoal gets extinguished as soon as it takes the pieces in its beak. Such myths are far from being true and may have arisen from the bird's habit of roosting in an open ground during the night. Perhaps, it might have arisen from its habit of feeding on Glow flies – *Jugnus*. The chakor's association with *Chandra*, or the moon, has inspired many poets, sages and romantic folklore in India.

In a deeper spiritual interpretation, Adi Shankracharya* compares Goddess Tripurasundari to the divinity of Goddess Amba's* smile that radiates cosmic consciousness and drips with the nectar of immortality in the face of a full moon. The chakor longs to immerse itself in the charm of Goddess Amba's smile and drink the nectar, intoxicated with the fulfilment of the purpose of its life. Here, while describing the charm of Goddess Tripurasundari, Adi Shankracharya has elevated the chakor's stature to a spiritual and divine pedestal.

HOW THE CHAKOR HAS BEEN GLORIFIED IN POETRY AND FOLK SONGS

The chakor has been glorified by many poets and in many folk songs. Some beautiful examples have been explained below.

IN THE WORDS OF KABIR

'Gahi tek chhorai nahi, jibh chonch jari jai;

Aiso tapt angar hai, tahi chakor chabai.'

According to Kabir, the legendary chakor gets so mesmerised on seeing the moon that it forgets all its pains and adores the moon. Similarly, people should be firm in their vows as life is not a bed of roses; however, this should not prevent them from following a spiritual path.

IN DOGRI FOLK SONGS

The Dogra are a tribe of people found predominantly in the North of India. For Dogri* women, life in the mountains is hard and lonely with long spells of separation from their soldier husbands and brothers. Their desire for reunion with their beloved ones resonates in their songs of separation, and the chakor – known for its yearning for the moon – deeply influences their folk songs. One such example has been translated:

The chakors call through the moonlight; listen to the chakoras in the moonlight;

calling to each other, see how the separated lovers pine for each other, but alas, my beloved comes not to me.

IN THE WORDS OF SURDAS

'Chatak kokil kir chakora, kujat vihang natat kal mora'

The manner in which 'chatak,' or the Pied Cuckoo, yearns for raindrops to quench its thirst, and the chakor yearns for the moon, my heart too yearns for you, Krishna my Lord.

IN PUNJABI LYRICS OF PRESENT DAY

The chakor continues to immortalise love even in present-day love songs and lyrics, as observed in the Punjabi album *Nai Jeena* by Nirmal Sidhu.

'Main tere dil da raja meri tu ban ja rani,

Tu chan e main chkor meri tere hath dor,

Tu chan e main chkor meri tere hath dor,

Saanu lageya ishq kamina soniya nai jeena,

Ni tere bin nai jeena soniya nai jeena'

(I am the king of your heart, hence be my queen, You are the moon, and I am chakor,

And my life is now in your hands,

We are infected with love for each other,

I cannot live without you; I cannot live without you.)

IN UTTAR PRADESH FOLKLORE

The chakor has a symbolic depiction in folk songs in *Brij bhasha**
– a language spoken in southwest Uttar Pradesh. In the song,
the gopis are found complaining about the mischievous Krishna
who troubles the gopis and prevents them from doing their daily
chores. In the song, Krishna is likened to the chakor that keeps
watching the moon at night as if it is in love with it. The song
describes the manner in which Krishna stares at the gopis.

'Neer bharan ko jab jab jaaun taakey chandra chakor,

Aate jaate rok le rastaa na maane chit chor,

Dhaaga ho to tor bhi daaloon, preet pe kis ka jor,

O maiyyaa chhede beech bajaar,

Ab mein kaa boloon sarkaar,

Ab mein kaa boloon'

(Whenever I go to fill water at the river,

He (Krishna) stares at me like how the chakor stares at the moon,

He blocks my way, doesn't let me pass,

The stealer of the hearts,

I would have broken it if it was a mere thread,

But then, who has control over the matters of heart?

He troubles me in the market,

And now what is there left for me to say?)

IN CHANCHARI FOLKSONG OF KUMAON AND GHARWAL

'Rajula jan Rani,

Kela jan Hateli,

Kaiki sua holi ini taprandi Chakor.'

(Queen as Rajula,

Whose hand as banana,

Whose lover would be as the chakor.)

IN MODERN HINDI POETRY

In Sufi mystic Malik Mohammed Jayasi's *Chayyavad** – in which Mirabai* yearns for Krishna while roaming through Brindavan in search for her ultimate union with Krishna – the chakor is depicted as a symbol, and it highlights the mystical bondage that the chakor has with the moon. One such translation is as follows:

'If thou are a hill, then I am your "Peacock,"

If thou are the Moon, then I am your "Chakor,"

If thou are a place of pilgrimage, then I am your pilgrim,

I have joined true love with thee'

IN BOLLYWOOD LYRICS

The chakor, as a legend of love, has been adopted from our rich Indian folklore and folk songs by Bollywood in its music, lyrics and themes. It has been mentioned in many songs, but the one sung by Mukesh in the film *Lal Bangla* immortalises it like none other. 'Chand' and 'chakor' have both been used as symbols of the lover and the loved.

'Chaand ko kyaa maaloom,

Ki chaahtaa hai use koyi chakor,

Wo bechaaraa door se dekhe,

Kare na koyi shor,

Door se dekhe aur lalchaaye,

Pyaas nazar ki badhati jaaye,

Badli kyaa jaane hai paagal,

Kiske man kaa mor.'

(The Moon knows not that the chakor yearns for him silently,

It yearns for the moon from a distance,

And the urge for it is ever increasing.

The cloud that hides the moon does not know

Whose heart is yearning for the moon.)

CHAKOR: IN ORNITHOLOGY

The chakor – belonging to the family of partridges – is widely spread in the North along the Himalayan range, commencing from Nepal to the Western Himalayas and extending up to Pakistan, Afghanistan, Iran, Turkey and Israel. It is found in dry, open and rocky hillsides with grass and sparse bushes and near cultivation areas and at heights extending from 3,000 feet to 16,000 feet. It feeds on a wide variety of seeds and insects. The chakor is found in coveys of 10 and in larger numbers of up to 50 birds.

Male chakors are monogamous, and the pairs nest on the ground in clutches of 7 to 14 eggs. Easy to domesticate, it can lay an egg a day throughout the breeding season while in captivity. Its quick flight, steep habitat and habit of running effortlessly make it the most challenging hunt of the game birds. Chakors are also preferred as cage and fighting birds because of their pugnacious behaviour.

OWLS

Hindi: Ghughu, Ullu, Khusat, Oolloo, Khakusat

Sanskrit: Uluk, Pechak, Ullookacheti (for Owlet)

Owls are mysterious and intelligent birds and are synonymous with fear and wisdom. They are both despised and admired in Indian folklore and are subject to many contradictory beliefs. While many see them as a sign of wealth, others consider them an ill omen and relate them to misfortune and death. Some even consider them foolish. In many parts of the country, they are associated with *tantriks**, black magic and witchcraft.

HOW ULUKA BECAME LAKSHMI'S MOUNT

Goddess Lakshmi, the consort of Lord Vishnu, is the Hindu goddess of wealth and prosperity and is also known as the *Ulkavahini*, or the one that rides *Uluka* or the owl. She is believed to bestow fortune, wealth, power and spiritual riches on her worshippers when mounted on an owl. In Bengal, the owl is known as *pechaka*, and it is worshipped during Lakshmi Puja.

Lord Jagannath, Lord Krishna's deity in Puri, Orissa, is also known as *Chokadola* or the lord with circular eyes, and he is speculated to be a manifestation of an owl that represents Lakshmi's consort, Vishnu.

'Uluka' in Sanskrit is also the name for Indra – the chief of all demigods and the lord of the heavens. It personifies wealth, courage, glory and power. The belief of Lakshmi riding on Indra and of him being compared to the incorrigible and the partly blind owl is to caution the seekers of the hazards of pursuing secular wealth instead of spiritual wealth. *Uloo* is a common expression in Hindi used for a foolish person.

HOW THE OWL IS DEPICTED AS THE MANIFESTATION OF THE INAUSPICIOUS ALAKSHMI

In contradiction to the general belief, many interpret the owl as a representation of Alakshmi – the goddess of inauspiciousness – the sister and the opposite form of Lakshmi. Alakshmi personifies and breeds strife, poverty, jealousy and decay. The owl is also considered to be a representation of Lord Vishnu, though this is strongly denied by traditionalists who believe that Lakshmi cannot ride on her own husband. Therefore, the owl can only accompany Goddess Lakshmi and not be ridden by her. Hence, the owl can only be a manifestation of Alakshmi. The interpretation is further reinforced with the argument that the inauspicious Alakshmi cannot be portrayed along with Lakshmi; hence, it has been chosen to be represented in the form of an owl.

THE SIGNIFICANCE OF OWLS IN THE MAHABHARATA AND THE RAMAYANA

Owls are known for their animosity with crows, and the crow-killing habit of the Dusky Horned Owl is legendary. There are references to owls in the great epics Mahabharata and Ramayana that indicate how the discreet ways of an owl can influence human beings' thinking.

In the Mahabharata, it was Ashwathama* who decided to carry out a successful and discreet midnight attack on the camp of the Pandavas* while they were asleep. He did this after having witnessed an owl creating terror and destruction amongst crows during the night.

In the Ramayana, after Vibhishana* abandoned Ravana, Sugreeva* – the brother of Bali – cautioned him against the owl-like tactics of Ravana.

WHY THE WISE OLD OWL IS CONSIDERED A GOOD OMEN

In the *Bhagavad Gita*, the owl personifies an enlightened person who resists the temptations of going awry on being bestowed with wealth and glory. It is symbolic of spiritual wisdom and signifies a person who optimises the use of wealth in a positive manner. For a person to see an owl in a dream, it is said to be symbolic of wisdom, foresight, vision and virtue.

In Orissa and Bengal, the iconic images of Lakshmi are accompanied by the image of a white owl, and hence, the visit by a white owl to a house is considered a good omen and signifies the flow of wealth and money. The owl also symbolises intelligence and penetrating sight.

Many read the 'hom hom' call of an owl as auspicious, as the call is related to their mating desire.

WHY OWLS ARE CONSIDERED AN ILL OMEN

Owls are nocturnal and birds of the night; they prefer to live in heavily wooded jungles, cemeteries and graveyards. They take shelter in the cavities or hollows of large trees and are believed to possess the spirits of departed souls. They are synonymous with death and darkness and are considered an ill omen. Their eerie midnight calls only add to this belief, and the superstitions vary from tribe to tribe, region to region and for different occasions. Such beliefs are, however, without any scientific logic.

SUPERSTITIONS ATTACHED TO OWLS

The Indo-Aryans considered the hooting of the owl as an ill omen.

In Meghalaya*, the Garo Hill tribes refer to owls as *doang* and relate its call to death. In other regions of the country, the owl perched on the roof of a house signifies misfortune; a call from the roof portrays the death of the owner. Seeing a dead owl in dreams signifies escape from ill health and death. As per the *Garuda Purana, Kaushika Mitrahanta* means a person who kills a friend and is reborn as an owl, cursed to kill innocent birds all his life.

In certain regions, parts of an owl's body are eaten for medicinal purposes, including as a cure for seizures. It is widely believed that eating owl eyes makes one's eyesight better such that one can see in the dark too. Their meat is also eaten to cure diseases. During Kali Puja, business communities in Bengal sacrifice owls to gain wealth.

HOW OWLS ARE USED IN RITUALS AND BLACK MAGIC PRACTISED BY TANTRIKS

To appease Goddess Lakshmi, there is a misbelief that sacrificing an owl, especially horned owls, during the period from *Sharad Purnima* – full moon night following *Dussehra** – to the day of *Diwali* brings wealth, wisdom, good luck and prosperity. Owl trappers have a lucrative trade by trapping and selling owls at exorbitant prices, leading to the death of a large number of owls during the season.

Even spotted owlets are not spared; they are given artificial 'ear tufts' or horns by binding their feathers with latex. Red chemical dye is injected into their eyes, and their bodies are dyed with *kaajal* or the lamp-black, prepared in a mustard oil base.

In black magic rituals and witchcraft, tantriks use various body parts of owls such as skulls, bones, eyes, beaks, kidneys and even eggshells. They prescribe broth prepared from owl eyes for curing children suffering from seizures. Owl meat is believed to have aphrodisiac properties and is eaten as a cure for infertility, to fulfil the desire for a male child and to treat rheumatism amongst children. It is also used by tantriks for '*vashikaran*,' i.e., for possessing individuals.

OWL: IN ORNITHOLOGY

Owls are nocturnal, silent and solitary 'birds of prey' that primarily feed on small mammals, rodents, birds and insects. Some even feed on fish. Despite being seen by many as a bad omen in Indian mythology, they are nature's great natural pest controllers and are great friends of the farmers. They help to maintain a balance in nature's food chain and are major contributors towards our ecology. Their vision, hearing capabilities, claws, feathers and beaks are structured to make them perfect hunting machines. Owls have a phenomenal capacity to see in the dark and can also see behind their own shoulders. They have strong hearing capabilities and use their facial discs to capture and redirect the sound waves of their prey to their ears.

The sharp, hawk-like beaks and powerful claws of the owl help in tearing the flesh of their prey. It is then swallowed and digested, while the undigested food such as bones and fur are regurgitated and ejected by an owl in the form of pellets.

There are as many as 32 different species of owls and owlets in India as appended in Krys Kazmierczak's *Birds of India*, including the ones in the Andaman and Nicobar Islands. The smallest owl found in India is the Collared Pigmy Owlet (*Glaucidium brodiei*). It is about 17 cms and the size of a quail. It is found in the Himalayas and the North East hills. The largest owl found in

India is the Forest Eagle Owl (*Bubo nipalensis*); it is about 63 cms and is larger than a buzzard.

Despite the protection accorded to it under the Wild Life (Protection) Act of 1972, the persecution of owls due to myths and superstitions, the practice of black magic by tantriks, their capture and sacrifice during the Diwali festival, the loss of their habitat, the cutting down of trees and the indiscriminate use of pesticides are only some of factors that have led to the drastic fall in the numbers of these amazing hunting birds in India. Time calls for serious efforts to protect their habitat. Severe penalties should be imposed against those persecuting them due to superstitions and misbeliefs.

CROWS

Hindi : Kowaa, Desi Kowwa

Sanskrit: Kaak, Kakol, Atmaghosh, Karat, Chirjeevin, Maukuli

If men had wings and bore black feathers,

Few of them would be clever enough to be crows.

– Henry Ward Beecher

Crows are fascinating and clever birds that demonstrate complex behaviour and are birdwatchers' delight. They are admired for their intelligence and would continue to be despised for being cunning, crafty and wicked, but for Salim Ali, the legendary ornithologist: 'Crows are really beautiful birds, and it all depends on how you look at them.' They are resourceful, omnivorous, adaptable and efficient scavengers that have strong survival traits and live in a social environment. They even mourn the death of their loved ones and play a critical role in maintaining environmental balance. The collective noun for crows is 'murder.'

Viewed both as a good and bad omen, crows have been marginalised, morally degraded and even considered inauspicious and evil by the Vedic Indians. Ominous and not highly revered in Indian mythology, they nevertheless enjoy special status. They are evocative of ancestors in Hinduism and are fed elaborately during Śrāddha – the period of remembrance – when Hindus recall their departed ancestors. In the *Agni Purana**, the King is advised to be as suspicious as a crow as a part of his *rajdharma**.

For the Shepherds of Kangra, the crow is a messenger who knows all about the past and the future and its cawing in the morning announces the arrival of a guest at home on that day.

AS SHANI'S VAHANA

In Indian mythology, Lord Shanidev is the protector of property and represses thievery. With the crow as his mount, it symbolises repression and control of evil traits such as thievery, of which the crow is representative and well known.

Shani Dev with the crow as his vahana

HOW KAAG BHUSUNDI BECAME A CROW

Kaag Bhusundi – as narrated in the *Uttar Kand Ramayan** – was a Brahmin* and a great devotee of Lord Rama who had migrated to the forests to live with the sages after the death of his parents. Being an ardent devotee of Lord Rama, he refused to believe the sages when they preached that God was formless. He argued that God existed only in the form of Lord Rama. This annoyed the sages who then cursed him into becoming a crow. Later, regretting their action, the sages showed mercy on Kaag Bhusundi and blessed him with a boon that his place of meditation, the *Kalptaru Tree**, would be a wish-fulfilling tree.

As per the legend, Vishnu's mount Garuda was sent for counselling to Kaag Bhusundi by Lord Brahma on the advice of sage Narada*, as Garuda had become increasingly arrogant after rescuing Lord Rama from the clutches of Meghnad* – who had earlier tied Lord Rama with the snake *Nagpaash* during the battle with Ravana. Garuda, who had started questioning Lord Rama's divinity, was advised by Kaag Bhusundi that salvation could be achieved only at the feet of Lord Rama.

As the story goes, Kaag Bhusundi in the form of a crow was playing with Lord Rama who was in the form of a child, and he picked a piece of bread from Lord Rama's hand. On losing the bread, Lord Rama started crying, thus casting doubts in the mind of Kaag Bhusundi of Lord Rama's cosmic powers. A disappointed Kaag Bhusundi flies away over the mountains and the oceans. Lord Rama who regrets losing a dedicated devotee follows Kaag Bhusundi through the cosmic world and expresses his affection for Kaag Bhusundi. On realising the truth of Lord Rama's divinity, Kaag Bhusundi asks for forgiveness. Lord Vishnu acknowledges the wisdom and intelligence of Kaag Bhusundi for being able to recognise him and grants him immortality and the boon that crows would be the last of the species to be wiped out during the *pralaya** or the deluge.

CROWS IN THE RAMAYANA

In Valmiki's Ramayana, Indra's son Jayanta who assumes the form of a crow is punished for insulting Sita and, in the bargain, loses one of his eyes. Ever since, a crow has to turn his head to look sideways to observe things below or above, and this behaviour is considered indicative of the crow's cunning, wickedness and even thievery.

In another version, Lord Rama is angered by Jayanta's insult of Sita and converts a blade of grass into a *Brahmastra** and draws it towards him. To escape Lord Rama's wrath, the crow is left with no other option but to surrender an eye. Hence, the crow has to turn and twist its neck every time to see things.

WHY CROWS ARE FED DURING ŚRĀDDHA

In Hindu mythology, it is believed that crows represent *aakash** and are carriers of the food for deliverance to the departed souls of one's ancestors and relations. Crows are seen as a symbol for caution. They warn people of coming dangers and are thus seen in the role of preservers and protectors. Hence, Hindus feed crows during different rituals. They are fed with rice and black lentils and other specially prepared food and sweets during the period of remembrance, i.e., Śrāddha or *Pitr Paksh** every year as part of *Tarpan** or *Pind daan**. On completion of the rituals, after the offerings, the remaining food is then distributed amongst the Brahmins along with clothes. The above ritual has also led to the idiom in Hindi '*shraadh ka kauwa,*' implying a particular individual who is commonly ignored but is given importance only when found to be of some benefit.

Similarly, crows are also fed at cremation grounds during cremations and later during the collection of ashes.

R K LAXMAN AND CROWS

Famous Indian cartoonist R K Laxman has spent a lifetime drawing and observing crows. For him, a 'house crow' is a very uncommon bird and the only bird that he can watch. He finds all other birds rather dull. He finds them to be immensely intelligent, sharp, lively, clever, cunning and cautious with strong survival instincts and having a nature very similar to human beings. He often painted their antics, and every crow he has painted has a human expression. For him, painting crows is a constant source of inspiration and relaxation.

Once, when asked to compare crows with politicians, he quipped: 'Are you mad? Crows are so good looking, so intelligent. Where will I find characters like that in politics?'

THE INTELLIGENCE OF CROWS

Crows are fascinating, remarkably intelligent and have good memories. They are shy, resourceful, extremely observant and even mischievous. They are the Einsteins of the avian world. In Indian literature, folktales are live with tales illustrating their intelligence. In the popular Panchatantra, Jataka and other children's tales namely *The Black Snake, Kalia the Crow* or *Thirsty Crow and the Pitcher,* the crow pre-empts evil designs, cautions and rescues other animals from danger and exudes wisdom, shrewdness and even the cunningness for which they are so famous.

Scientists have carried out research, conducted experiments and found that crows can plan and communicate with individuals, can be taught to speak words and short sentences, can live in hierarchic societies and have rivalries with ravens. They can remember human faces and differentiate one human face from another and even hold grudges.

They have the ability to innovate and fabricate tools and bend wires to obtain food; they can also remove grubs from logs with fabricated tools and use bread crumbs as baits for fishing. Their capacity to be innovative is a trait sufficiently highlighted in *The Crow and the Pitcher* story. They have been observed to drop nuts with hard shells on a heavy traffic street so that they can be crushed open by passing traffic, and synchronise the retrieval of these nuts with the pedestrian lights. Ever noticed how they can collectively react with vengeance if harmed?

AND, ABOUT... SCARECROWS

Crows are notorious for the extensive damage they cause to seeded fields by picking freshly sown seeds in the fields. To ward off the menace, farmers have resorted to raising decoys as 'scarecrows' in their fields. They used traditional human figures, mannequins, helmets and even human skulls to ward off the crows, all of which have only proven to be ineffective. Farmers have now switched to more modern gadgets like shimmering PET films, water sprays and automatic gun noises powered by propane gas.

Interestingly, the scarecrow has developed into multiple themes such as movies, songs and even festivals. Many believe that scarecrows are more for warding off evil spirits than crows.

CROWS AND THE DALAI LAMAS

The crow, amongst the Buddhists in Tibet, is believed to be the incarnation of the *Mahakala* or *The Great Black One* – the protector of the monasteries in Tibet. The Mahakala is believed to have appeared before Ngawang Drakpa, the founder and builder of the Dhe-Tsang monastery in eastern Tibet in the year 1414 in the form of a crow to guide him to the location where the monastery was to be constructed. The crow lifted his scarf and dropped it on a Juniper tree, and that is where the Dhe-Tsang monastery stands today, built around the Juniper tree.

As the legend has it, the house of the First Dalai Lama, *Chokey Geundun or Kundun*, was attacked by bandits when he was a little baby, forcing the family to flee and abandon the little baby behind. On their return, they found a pair of crows guarding the baby. Ever since, crows are linked with the Dalai Lama and are one of the symbols of his rank. A pair of crows was observed outside the house of the present Dalai Lama following the morning he was born, and they would visit the house every morning. Similar observations, as reported by the present Dalai Lama, Tenzin Gyatso, were also made during the births of the first, seventh, eighth and twelfth Dalai Lamas.

CROWS: IN ORNITHOLOGY

Crows belong to the family *Crovidae* and genus *Crovus*. They are the largest of the *Passerines* birds. They have a highly developed mental and complex social organisation and perhaps are the most familiar birds in India. They are highly gregarious, bold and aggressive, audacious, cunning and uncannily wary. In India, the genus includes the Jungle Crow, the Raven and the Jackdaw.

Crows are omnivores, and their food intake includes small invertebrates, fruits, seeds, termites, locusts, eggs, kitchen scrap and dead rats. They even scavenge on carcasses. While they are great contributors towards the cleaning of the environment and hence are more of friends than enemies to the farmers, they are also a major threat to other smaller birds in cities and towns. A dissection of their stomachs revealed that their diet constituted 99% of insects, including crop-damaging insects. Their love for corn is well known, and their capacity to damage freshly sown seeds in the fields had resulted in the innovation of scarecrows by farmers.

Crows are monogamous, and both the sexes look alike. They build nests on high treetops, in the hollows of trees and on manmade structures and their simple nests are made up of sticks and twigs intermixed with mud, coir fibres, etc. One may even be fascinated to discover scrap pieces of wires and caps of Soda water bottles.

There is growing concern over the dwindling numbers of these highly adaptive birds from our neighbourhood. Increasing urbanisation, coupled with the extensive use of insecticides, deforestation and climatic changes, has seen a drastic decline in their numbers over the years. Can you imagine your lives without the wicked-eyed crow keeping an eye on you?

CRANES

Hindi: Kurunch, Kurch, Saras, Karkara

Sanskrit: Neelang, Pushkrah

Through millennia, cranes – the largest of all the flying birds – have been regarded as a symbol of good fortune, fidelity, happiness and longevity. They are elegant, imposing and majestic, and the devotion of the pair for one another has caused them to be venerated and has earned them a sacred and supernatural status in Indian culture and folklore.

In Gujarat, it is customary to take newlywed couples to see a pair of Sarus cranes for a long and happy conjugal life. The elaborate courtship dance of the cranes adds to their symbolic stature and has inspired many a poet. Kalidasa makes a mention of them in his sensuous *Meghdootam*, while Valmiki was inspired to write the *Ramayana* after he saw, with dismay, a fowler knocking down a crane during its spectacular courtship dance with its mate. Emperor Jehangir, in his memoirs, observed and wondered at the devotion of a Sarus crane that refused to abandon the remains of its mate.

In Northern India, feminine beauty is compared to the Demoiselle crane or *koonj* because of its grace and elegance. In the Mahabharata, there are many references to cranes. In the battle against the Kauravas, the army of the Pandavas adopted the *Kaunchvuh* formation based on the V-form of the cranes while in flight. In Panchatantra and Jataka stories too, cranes form the central characters of many stories such as *The Crane and the Crab*, *Foolish Crane and the Mongoose* and *Lion and the Crane*. Known to be good watchdogs, cranes have been kept as pets even by royalty in their palaces.

SAGE VALMIKI, THE SARUS CRANE (KRAUNCH) AND THE RAMAYANA

In search for a man with all the virtues of a noble soul, Valmiki – a robber who turned into a sage – asked Narada if he knew of any such person. Narada narrated the story of Lord Rama to him and predicted that Sita would soon come seeking shelter in his hermitage. Valmiki then left for the land of the *Tamsa River*. On a winter morning, while he was on the banks of the river, he was awestruck at the sight of a pair of Sarus cranes performing their courtship dance. Soon, much to his grief and dismay, a fowler fatally wounded the female with his arrow. The plight of the surviving Sarus so anguished Valmiki that he lamented a curse on the fowler that he shall not live long for having killed a bird while it was making love, thus breaking his vow of non-violence. Valmiki soon realised that his curse was actually a poetic verse:

Manishada pratish tatum samagah ssashvat Issamah yat krouncha mithunadekam sokam avadhim kama mohitam.

(O fowler, you would not live for long. Why did you cruelly kill the innocent male crane when it was making love to its partner. As you have dealt a death blow to one of the two cranes which was most innocent and not deserving of this harm, I utter this word of immediate annihilation of yourself.)

He went back to his hermitage and asked his disciple to memorise it. Later, while he was meditating and brooding over the killing of the Saras, Lord Brahma appeared before him and acknowledged to Valmiki that it was he who had enabled him to translate his grief into melodic composition or *kavvaya*. He asked Valmiki to compose the Ramayana, which is the story of Ram and Sita, the two lovers who are forced to part time and again.

Sage Valmiki, the fowler and the cranes

PUTANA AS THE VAKI CRANE

Putana*, a *rakshasi*, demoness, is summoned by Kansa*, the King of Vrindavana, and assigned the job of breastfeeding and poisoning infant Krishna. She is also portrayed as a *Vaki*, a female crane, symbolising hypocrisy, crookedness and the desire for the materialistic world.

THE CRANE SEEKS ANSWERS FROM YUDHISHTIR ON DHARMA

One day, during the Pandavas twelve-year exile in the forest, Yudhishtir* – the eldest amongst the Pandavas – asked Nakula – the youngest of his brothers – to go out and fetch water from a nearby lake with crystal clear water. Just as he was about to draw water to drink, Nakula heard a voice asking him not to draw water without answering his questions first. Nakula, who was too impatient to quench his thirst, disregarded the warning and soon fell dead. As time lapsed, Yudhishtir sent his brothers Sahadeva*, Bhima* and Arjuna* – one after the other – to fetch water and also to inquire about the fate of their brothers. As the brothers failed to return, Yudhishtir became anxious and decided to go out in search of them himself.

On reaching the lake, Yudhishtir discovered the inevitable. Just as he started to grieve and lament over the death of his brothers, he heard the same voice call out, disguised as a *Baka* (crane), 'I am Dharma, the *Yaksha*,* and it is me who has led your brothers to this fate. You, Yudhishtir, too shall meet the same fate if you fail to answer my questions before drawing water from the lake.' Yudhishtir agreed to answer the questions based on his intelligence and philosophy. Yudhishtir went on to aptly answer the eighteen questions that are appended in the Mahabharata as *Dharm-Baka Upakhyan* – the Legend of the Virtuous Crane – and thus brought all his brothers back to life.

I AM NO CRANE - THE STORY OF KAUSHIKA AS TOLD BY SAGE MARKANDEYA TO YUDHISHTIR

Sage Markandeya* and Yudhishtir were once discussing the virtues of the fairer sex, who they said was sacrificing, generous and forgiving in nature – quite the opposite to a treacherous and neglecting husband. It was then that Sage Markandeya narrated the story of a Brahmin named Kaushika who, by his very looks and in a fit of anger, killed a crane for dirtying his head with its dropping while it was sitting in a tree above him. A little later, Kaushika went out to seek alms from the households. He placed a curse on a housewife who made a delay in offering alms to him as she was dutifully attending to her sick husband. The lady, while asking for forgiveness, reminded Kaushika that she was no crane as she was delayed while honestly performing her duty as a wife. That, Sage Markandeya said was the true worship of God.

THE SIGNIFICANCE OF CRANES IN CHRISTIANITY

Cranes are revered in Christianity as symbols of vigilance and foresight; they are considered to be the natural enemies of the devil because of their ability to kill snakes.

Cranes have the capacity to endure long journeys during migration. Hence, they are symbols of endurance, and their return during the spring is seen as Christ's resurrection.

On the contrary, Christian legend has it that anyone showing disrespect to a saint or committing a sin shall be transformed into a crane.

Christianity also preaches that Christians should remain alert and watchful against committing sins, much in the same manner as the crane that holds a stone in its raised foot so as to avoid falling asleep.

CRANES IN PANCHATANTRA AND JATAKA TALES

Cranes commonly appear in the age-old Panchatantra and Jataka fables of the Rig Veda era and 4th century BC respectively, wherein the birds and the animals speak and behave like humans and impart wisdom to a child who reads it. Besides the imparted wisdom, the stories are also reflective of the traits, personalities and the characteristics of the birds and the animals portrayed – as perceived by the story writers – though the perception may or may not be accurate.

In Panchatantra and Jataka stories, namely *The Foolish Crane and the Mongoose, Wolf and the Crane, Farmer and the Crane, Crane and the Crab,* a crane is depicted as cunning, wily, tricky, non-trusting and even foolish and innocent.

CRANES: IN ORNITHOLOGY

Cranes belong to the family *Gruidae*; they are stately, charismatic and majestic birds with spectacular courtship displays that help pairs to synchronise their mating postures. The elaborate displays are also territorial. Their anatomy is so structured that their sonorous and far-reaching trumpets can be heard up to several kilometres. Primarily birds of shallow wetlands, cranes are opportunistic feeders and forage on anything from berries, seeds, nuts, fruits, tubers and rhizomes to insects, snails, molluscs, small mammals, reptiles, small fish and amphibians. They can also migrate long distances in search of food.

Gregarious by nature, cranes are largely monogamous and commonly seen in pairs. They pair for life, contrary to the belief that they change mates, or even divorce, if initial attempts to breed fail. They remain paired as long as they are breeding successfully. They are terrestrial; they nest on the ground in reed beds or around shallow water with nests made of vegetative matter. They lay between 2 and 3 eggs, and their chicks are nidifugous and become active in a short while after hatching. The parents are often seen protecting their juveniles on the flanks by keeping them in the centre while foraging.

During migration, cranes gather in large social groups and fly at altitudes exceeding 18,000 ft. They fly in 'V' formations for greater efficiency and also to conserve energy. They frequently change leaders during long flights, as the leader alone has to confront the heavy wind resistance while the others make the best of the draught produced by the wings of the birds ahead of them. Fighter aircrafts also follow a similar formation pattern during flights to conserve fuel.

India plays host to six of the fifteen species of cranes found across the globe. All the species found in India are migratory except for the Sarus crane, which is residential and is spread all over the Indian peninsula with a large concentration of its population in Uttar Pradesh. Details of some of the most common cranes in India are as follows:

1. Siberian crane (*Grus leucogeranus*): Listed as critically endangered under the *International Union for Conservation of Nature* (IUCN) Red list, they migrate in winters from their breeding grounds in Russia to the Keoladeo Ghana National Park at Bharatpur. The number of birds visiting Bharatpur has dwindled over the years, and the last of the Siberian cranes visited the Bharatpur bird sanctuary in 2002.

2. Demoiselle crane (*Antropoides virgo*): Also known as *koonj* in Hindi, it is one of the most beautiful and the smallest of the cranes. They migrate from Mongolia

and China via Afghanistan and Pakistan to India. Enroute, they are subject to persecution and hunting by traditional crane hunters. The Pathan tribesmen of the Kurram Valley – in Pakistan's legendary North West Frontier Province – hunt migrating Demoiselle and common cranes by using decoy cranes and coiled nylon or handwoven cords called *soiias* with lead weights at one end. On the contrary, their migration to Khichan in Rajasthan is an annual spectacle where the villagers accord protection and feed the large congregations of Demoiselle cranes.

3. Common crane (*Grus grus*): It breeds in the wetlands of the northern parts of Europe and Asia. The Asian population migrates in winters to Banni grasslands and Kutch in Gujarat, where nearly 30 different sites exist. An estimated 40,000 and 75,000 birds visit Banni and Kutch respectively. With *Prosopis juliflora,* an invasive weed, increasingly spreading in the grasslands, it is likely to adversely affect the ecology of the grasslands, thereby impacting the future of the common crane in the area.

4. Hooded crane (*Grus monacha*): It breeds in southeastern Russia and Northern China and the non-breeding flocks occur in the Russia-Mongolia-China border region; they are vagrant visitors in North East India.

5. Black-necked Crane (*Grus nigricollis*): Rather elusive, but not adversely threatened, the black- necked crane was discovered in 1876 by Russian naturalist Nikolay Przhevalsky in the tablelands of Central Asia and the plateau of eastern Ladakh, southern Tibet, Bhutan and Arunachal Pradesh. It is deeply revered by the Ladakhis, who call it *Thrung Thrung Karmo* in their local language and only 3 to 4 pairs are known to breed within Indian

boundaries. In terms of folklore, the birds are sacred; they are considered to be the reincarnation of the sixth Dalai Lama that comes back to our world to help other souls attain enlightenment. It is, therefore, imperative that the ecology of these breeding sites are properly managed and protected.

6. Sarus Crane (*Grus antigone*): Resident and commonly seen in the countryside of Northern India, primarily in the state of Uttar Pradesh, the Sarus crane is deeply revered, and even tolerated by the locals who see it as a symbol of fidelity. Killing one is equivalent to killing a human being and, hence, it is accorded natural protection by the peasants. It is because of the status it enjoys that it has survived despite the rapid fall of its habitat. Bird of the marshlands, the Sarus crane is omnivorous and feeds on frogs, insects, aquatic and plant life. They are territorial, indulge in extensive courtship display and are aggressive towards any intruders.They nest on the ground in the middle of the wetlands and paddy fields on small islands. They lay 2 eggs and are model parents, for they zealously guard, walk and feed their chicks.

CONSERVATION

Cranes are accorded complete protection under the law in India, but despite the protection, their status continues to be threatened. Loss and degradation of the wetlands, indiscriminate use of pesticides, damage to the eggs of the Sarus cranes, hunting of migrating cranes along their route of migration and increasing levels of human disturbance are only some of the factors endangering the existence of the cranes in India.

PARROTS

Hindi: Tota, Tuiya

Sanskrit: Kinkiraat, Chimi, Chimik, Popat, Manjupathak, Vach, Raktatund

Popular as cage birds, parrots are highly intelligent and have the ability to mimic human speech and master many other skills. They have enjoyed a very visible presence through time immemorial in Indian fables, folklore, Jataka and Panchatantra stories and are depicted as agents of love, erotica, deception and even wisdom. In Indian mythology, the Rose-ringed parakeet is depicted as the mount or the vahana of the Hindu god of carnal love, Kamdev. The only female form of Lord Vishnu, Mohini – popularly known as the great enchantress – is also depicted holding a parrot in her hand, reinforcing the image of parrots as representatives of carnal love. In the Puranas, Kunjal, the parrot, is projected as an enlightened preacher of virtues.

In present-day India, roadside fortune tellers use parrots for picking up Tarot cards to predict the fortune of their clients, while farmers consider them as serious pests for causing severe damage to their fruit orchards and crops.

Kamdev, the God of Love on his mount the parrot

AS KAMDEV'S MOUNT

Parrots are commonly associated with erotica, love and romance as observed from many Indian tales such as the Śukasaptati or *Seventy Tales of the Parrot.* Their affectionate nature, as seen in their interactions with their own beings, their skill in mimicking human speech, their monogamous behaviour and their ability to be wise in the matters of the heart are some of the attributes that qualify them for being Kamdev's mount.

ŚUKASAPTATI OR THE SEVENTY TALES OF THE PARROT

Śukasaptati is a collection of 72 stories within stories, originally written in Sanskrit during the 12th Century. They are narrated to a woman by a pet parrot that is kept by her merchant husband to keep a watch on her nefarious and immoral activities while he is on his outstation business trips. The parrot narrates the stories to his mistress on 70 different nights and succeeds in preventing her from meeting her paramour. The tales depict situations that are ribald, erotic and even delve into areas of infidelity and incest. Few of the narrated stories such as *Tale of the Two Parrots* and *The King and the Parrots* have been picked up from Jataka and Panchatantra stories.

PARROTS IN THE PURANAS

In the Puranas, the wisdom of the parrots is illustrated in the form of an enlightened parrot, Kunjal, who is knowledgeable and has mastery over many scriptures and gives discourses to his young ones Ujjawal, Samujjwal, Vijjwal and Kapinjal. It teaches them the importance of practising abstinence and self-control and of having absolute devotion towards Lord Vishnu. Through the narration of these tales, Kunjal emphasised on virtues such as benevolence, truthfulness, meditation, the study of scriptures and respect towards the elders as a passage to heaven. Sage Chyavan*, who happened to be listening to these sermons while lying in the shade of a banyan tree, is awestruck at the knowledge of Kunjal the parrot.

THE PARROT WITH MATANGI, MEENAKSHI, SHUKAPRIYA OR GODDESS SARASWATI

Matangi is a tantrik manifestation of Saraswati and is said to be the daughter of the tribal or the low caste Chandals. The parrot is her celestial partner and is depicted to be seated on her right shoulder. Many interpret the parrot to be reciting in a human voice, imparting the 64 *bahyakalas** or skills such as singing, dancing, music, painting, craft, cooking, sewing, dressing, architecture, etc., to the goddess. Matangi is also known by the name of Shukapriya – or one fond of the parrot – and the parrot as her celestial partner signifies that it is imparting the knowledge of *Nada* or music or singing in tune with her veena and chanting the Vedas to the goddess. In many South Indian temples, Matangi, or Meenakshi, is depicted holding a parrot in her hand, which represents the powers of speech as being inherent in nature.

Goddess Meenakshi

THE PARROT OR KILI AT ARUNACHALESWARAR TEMPLE

As the legend has it, Saint Arunagirinathar – a devotee of Lord Murugan – had won a contest against a renowned orator Sambandan who, planning to take revenge, prompted the blind king into commissioning the services of Arunagirinathar by asking him to fetch the *Parijat** flower from the heavens for restoring his eyesight. Arunagirinathar entered the body of a dead parrot and flew off to the heavens, leaving his body behind in the Arunachaleswarar temple. Sambandan, sensing an opportunity, asked the king to have the body of Arunagirinathar cremated. On his return from the heavens with the Parijat flower, Arunagirinathar helped to restore the king's eyesight but realised soon that he could not re-enter the human body as the same had been cremated. He continued to live in the parrot's form without any regrets, writing poetry in praise of Lord Murugan for the rest of his life. An ornately painted statue of the parrot (Kili) can still be found to date in the Kili Gopuram tower at the Temple of the Arunachaleswarar.

PARROTS AT ADI ANNAMALAI TEMPLE

During the restoration of the Adi Annamalai Temple*, utmost care and precautions were taken to preserve the little openings on the top of the compound walls as nesting sites to help parrots, doves, pigeons, sparrows, owls and bats breed. Large flocks of parrots and doves can be seen even today during the nesting period.

Arunagirinathar depicted as a parrot (Kili) in the
Arunachaleswarar temple

PARROTS: MYTHS AND STORIES

There are many myths and stories associated with the parrot in Indian folklore and literature. Some of the stories have been listed below.

STORY OF PRINCESS LABAM

An Indian prince learns of a beautiful and mysterious Princess Labam from the King of Parrots, Hiraman, who can talk like human beings. The prince sets out to the forbidden land in search of the mysterious Princess Labam, whom he falls in love with. He eventually wins the hand of the princess after successfully overcoming numerous tests and challenges put before him by the princess's father. He is able to do this with the support of the animals and people that he had helped earlier when they were in distress. He succeeds in grinding 80 kgs of mustard seeds overnight with the help of the ants with whom he had earlier shared sweetmeats given to him by his mother. He is also able to kill two demons with the help of a tiger, and its mate, whom he had earlier helped when it was in distress by removing a painful thorn from its paw.

THE MERCHANT AND HIS CLEVER PARROT

An Indian merchant had a parrot as a pet in captivity. While leaving for business to a distant country, he asks his pet if it has any message to convey to his brethren. The parrot asks him to tell them that he is held captive and confined to a cage. The merchant, on reaching his destination, conveys the message to the first flock of parrots that he sees. Upon hearing his message, a parrot falls dead on the spot. This surprises the merchant and, after returning, he rebukes his pet parrot for having sent such an agonising message. On hearing of his brethren's death, the pet parrot too falls dead and leaves his master grieving for the loss. No sooner does the master take the dead parrot out of its cage than it flies off to its freedom, revealing that it had only faked its death as a means to escape from captivity.

THE TALE OF THE TWO PARROTS (JATAKA)

Two handsome and adventurous parrot brothers Radha and Potthapada are captured and caged in a golden cage by a king to entertain his courtiers. They live comfortable lives and are admired by the royal guests till one day when they are joined by an ugly ape Kalabahu. The ape becomes the centre of attraction for his antics, thus stealing all the attention away from the parrots. Jealous of the developments and the neglect, Potthapada is hurt and confides in Radha. Wiser of the two, Radha assures Potthapada that praise, blame, attention, honour and dishonour are only temporary facets and that the royal guests shall soon be disappointed with the ape's antics, and would get to know the parrots' true worth eventually. Soon, Kalabahu the ape starts to misbehave with the visitors and is sent back to the forest. Radha's predictions thus come true and the handsome brothers regain their lost glory.

DEATH AND LORD INDRA'S PARROT (PANCHATANTRA)

One day, Lord Indra, the lord of the heavens, was holding a *durbar** of all the gods in heaven when Yama, the lord of death, came to visit them. At that time, also perched with Lord Indra on his throne was his favourite parrot. Yama smiled on seeing the parrot and set him trembling in fear, for the parrot knew that his end had come nearer for sure. Upon sensing trouble for his pet, Lord Indra came to his rescue and pleaded with Yama to spare the parrot's life. Yama regretted that there was very little that he could do in the matter and asked Indra to speak to Destiny instead. Destiny too expressed her inability to help and instead directed them to Death, and the parrot died the instant Death set its eyes on him.

Yama walked up to Lord Indra and asked him to accept the ultimate truth of life as death was the final destiny of every living being.

The moral of this story is that *everyone who takes birth in this world has to die one day.*

A KING AND THE PARROTS

Two parrots were once captured by a tribal king. While one was kept as a pet by him, the other managed to escape only to be recaptured by a sage. They both picked up different value systems and responded differently when a neighbouring king visited them. While the tribal king's pet parrot misbehaved and responded rudely on seeing the king, the sage's parrot was both regardful and polite in the king's presence. The moral of the story is that *a man is known by the company he keeps.*

PARROTS: IN ORNITHOLOGY

Parrots are arboreal*, brightly coloured and generally green. They are vegetarian and feed largely on fruits, berries and grains and have short and strongly hooked beaks. They nest in tree holes, and their flight is graceful and swift. Large flocks can move through forest trees with amazing dexterity. Parrots are notoriously famous for the damage that large flocks can cause to standing crops and fruit orchards. Parrots also have great economic value for the role played by them in the dispersal of seeds.

India has nearly 12 different species of parrots, and they are a common sight in both urban and rural India. The decrease in their abundance in the recent years has raised concerns. Detailed studies need to be carried out and a database needs to be created to ascertain the cause of their decline. Shrinkage of their habitat, extensive use of pesticides and their popularity as cage birds are, for certain, the major causes for the decline in their numbers.

HOUSE SPARROW

Hindi: Gauriya, Churi, Khas Churi

Sanskrit: Ashvak, Ashvakchatak, Chatak

Sparrows (*Passer domesticus*) are a child's first encounter with birds. They are an embodiment of a wholesome life and are symbolised as the 'friendly spirits' of the household. They are also considered god's gift to mankind. Bubbly, spirited and energetic, the little sparrow in Salim Ali's words '… is a confirmed hanger-on of man,' while M Krishnan calls them 'companionable.' Many believe that sparrows bring good luck to the family if found to be nesting in one's house, and hence are well fed. In the past, housewives made *rangolis* in their courtyards with rice powder so that sparrows could feed on it. Many households still follow the ritual of offering the first bite of their meals to the diminutive bird.

Proud and hyperactive, these little birds have dotted every house in every neighbourhood and have carved a special place for themselves amongst *Homo sapiens*. They have inhabited their surroundings for centuries. In his book *Ghubar-e-khatir* – and the essay *Chirya Chiray ki kahani* – Mulana Azad Kalam confesses to having to surrender to a pair of determined house sparrows who decide to invade and nest in his jail room in Ahmednagar. He writes about their idiosyncrasies, their social behaviour and about the marital relations of individuals who compete amongst themselves to win over potential mates. He aptly describes the dominating male as a Mulla* for 'his argumentative, garrulous and quarrelsome behaviour,' while M Krishnan in *Of Birds and Birdsong* likens sparrows to the hearty 'objective' type of people in public who never blush and are 'vivacious, inquisitive, determined and wholly insensitive'; he also finds their chirping as 'pleasant, tinkling and repetitious.' Khushwant Singh observed that the chirping of the sparrows is 'proportionate' to the availability of food and is a balance between a sparrow's desire to keep food all to itself and its fear of predators.

Sparrows prefer to roost in plants with dense foliage such as the Jungle jalebi (*Pithecellobium dulce*), Madhumalti (*Combretum indicum*), Bamboo and Bougainvillea. They are particularly noisy while roosting and can be seen in large flocks akin to bee-like swarms during roosting time.

Forever vigilant, sparrows are gregarious and can be seen freely jumping, hopping and chirping around in our courtyards, rushing in to pick household leftovers and titbits trashed as kitchen waste as well as sievings of lentils and grains being readied for the daily meal. They establish their right as the primary occupants in our houses, gardens, courtyards, verandas and even make forced entries into our bedrooms. They nest in the upturned cup covers of ceiling fans, thus littering our living spaces with their nesting material. The whole house would end up mourning, even forsaking meals, if one of the birds injured itself from a rotating ceiling fan. They have been our constant companions, and their lively behaviour tends to constantly lift our spirits and beckon upon us to move on regardless of current circumstances.

Sparrows are compulsive urbanites and love urban spaces. They nest in wall crevices, holes and buildings and nest boxes put up by their human companions. Large populations are also found in the countryside next to human habitation. Their primary diet consists of seeds, berries and waste crumbs, while insects and worms are fed to freshly hatched chicks to supplement their high protein diet.

In Christianity, sparrows are seen as a symbol of God's presence and are frequently mentioned in the Bible. Considering their social behaviour, the sight of a lone sparrow is considered as a symbol of isolation and loneliness.

In Islam, seeing a sparrow in one's dream is considered a good omen and is interpreted as a sign of luxurious life, wealth and a high status in society.

In Panchatantra, using wisdom, tact and collective wit, a family of sparrows avenges the destruction of their nest by an elephant and manages to kill him with the help of a gnat, woodpecker and frog.

Held in great reverence across the country, villagers of Mohanpur in Banda District of Uttar Pradesh even perform a grand wedding of the *Chunmun* (male sparrow) and *Gauriya* (female sparrow) with the Chunmun riding a horse to the bride's house.

SPARROWS: IN ORNITHOLOGY

A sharp decline in the population of the sparrows in the recent years has been a major cause for concern for one and all. Loss of habitat, change in lifestyles and food habits, switching over to packaged foods, excessive use of pesticides, mushrooming of mobile towers, electromagnetic radiation, predation, pollution, dwindling forest cover and non-availability of insects are known to be the major contributory factors for their decline. Major rehabilitation efforts in towns and cities have seen the resurgence of sparrows in some pockets, but there is still a long way to go before we can see them bouncing back effectively.

CUCKOO

Hindi: Kapak, Upak, Papiya

Sanskrit: Anya Vapya, Kalkanth, Kinkir, Kinkirat, Kokil, Gandharv, Parpusht, Madhukanth, Madhughosh

Cuckoos are a part of many Indian legends and have deeply influenced Indian folklore, ancient Indian literature, poetry, folk songs and music. The cuckoo's melodious and sensuous voice inspired Kalidasa to make Papiha* and the *Vasanta ritu** the core theme of his writings *Shakuntala* and *Meghdootam*. They have also figured in Tansen's and Baiju Bawara's* musical creations. The cuckoo prominently appears not only in Punjabi, Bhojpuri, Bengali and other Indian tribal folk songs – dominating as a strong love symbol in folklore – but also in many Bollywood songs. In folklore in Mathura and other parts of Uttar Pradesh, they narrate a tale in which Lord Krishna is described as playing his flute along with the cuckoos under a *Kadam* tree.

In India, the cuckoo family has over 24 different species, including the Coucals. Barring a few exceptions, cuckoos are notoriously famous for brood parasitism; they do not build their own nests and instead, lay eggs in the nests of other birds and leave it upon them to incubate and rear their chicks. Brood parasitism is mentioned, as early as 2000 BC, in Sanskrit literature as *anya vapa* or 'the one raised by others.'

Cuckoos feed majorly on figs and caterpillars. They are capable of fulfilling most of their water requirements from their food intake, giving rise to the popular folklore belief that cuckoos drink only raindrops and are never seen to visit water to quench their thirsts. Besides, the breeding period of the cuckoos falls during the rainy season when the males are very vocal, and people read their persistent calls during the rainy season as an appeal to the clouds, seeking a few raindrops for their parched throats.

The cuckoo families, in addition to the species that have been named, also include the malkohas and coucals or crow pheasants that are non-parasitic.

KOEL

Hindi: *Koel*

The koel *(Eudynamys scolopacea)* is held in great reverence for its enchanting song by poets in ancient Indian literature and Sanskrit verses and is a favourite of many Indian poets. The commonest of the Indian cuckoos and the State bird of Pondicherry, the Asian koel is protected from harm by *Manusmriti** – an ancient legal text amongst the many *Dharmaśāstras** of Hinduism. It was one of the first Sanskrit texts translated during the British rule of India in 1794 by Sir William Jones and used to formulate the Hindu law by the colonial government.

Koel or *Kokila* is derived from Hindi and Sanskrit words that are onomatopoeic in origin. As per the popular phrase 'Thrice welcome darling of the spring,' the koel is also described as the *Vasanta Doot* or the invoker of spring. It is a popular belief that with the blossoming of the mango flowers, its call ushers the *Vasanta ritu* and weaves a web of excitement and emotion. It is believed to ignite desire in the hearts of separated lovers yearning for each other. The call of the koel is also a bioindicator, and it helps to predict the changes in the season.

Known for its voice that sounds sweet even to the gods, the koel has earned itself a dominating place in Indian literature, sayings and idioms. The charm of the koel's voice is aptly described in the following Sanskrit sentence taken out of the *Padma Purana**:

Kokilana rute punyae sarwatra madhurayte

The koel's voice – irrespective of it being called out in any emotion or sentiment – sounds so sweet that it charms everyone, even if it were the gods.

Its call *peekahan* is interpreted as 'Where is my beloved?' and in Marathi, it is *paos-ala,* i.e., 'The summer is coming.' Words like *Kokal baini* are used for describing the sweetness in the speech of a person, while the koel's black colour and distinctive red eyes associate it with fear and ugliness.

Koels also practice brood parasitism and are known as *Kakpusht* in Sanskrit, i.e., 'The one reared by crows.' They cheat and chase the otherwise intelligent crows out of their nests, while their opportunist females deviously enter and deposit eggs in the crows' nests. Other birds that suffer at the hand of the koels are drongos, magpies, mynas and babblers. Brood parasitism is also the reason why the koel is known by the name *Kakpitraswasa* or the 'crow's father's sister' in Sanskrit, based on the Indian practice where the sister leaves her children to be reared by her brother.

Apart from folklore and classical literature, the call of the koel has inspired many a song in Bollywood films and other regional films.

'Ku hu, ku hu bole koyaliya…'

'Koel ki kook nyaari, papiha ki bol pyari…'

'Sahio koel Hanju dolhe. Papiha wekho ni, Bherha pee-pee kar…'

(ku hu ku hu calls the koel,

her plaintive call is mellifluous, and the papiha's voice is full of sweetness,

the koel sings in doleful tears. Oh! Look at the papiha singing of separation from his beloved.)

– a Punjabi folksong

PIED CRESTED CUCKOO

Hindi: Papiya, Kala papiya, Chatak

Pied Crested Cuckoo (*Clamator jacobinus*) or the Monsoon Bird is a breeding visitor to Northern India and harbinger of monsoons to the country. India has two varieties – the smaller one is a permanent resident of South India and Sri Lanka, while the larger ones migrate to Northern India, coinciding with the onset of the Southwest Monsoon in June and depart in October after the monsoon retreats – presumably for South Africa with their young ones reared by their foster parents.

Referred to as *chatak* by Kalidasa in his famous *Meghdootam*, the Pied Crested cuckoo is commonly mentioned in Indian poetry as a bird with a beak on its head – probably for the prominent crest on its head – that guides the monsoon clouds and waits for the rains to quench its thirst. Kalidasa also mentions the Pied Crested cuckoo as *Sardang chatak* and *Divaukas* in *Shakuntala*, where King Dushyant encounters the *Divaukas* or the one living in the heavens above the clouds during his journey to *Indralok* in his chariot. Its absence from the country during the spring coincides with King Dushyant's stay above the clouds in the heavens.

COMMON HAWK CUCKOO (HIEROCCYCX VARIUS) OR BRAIN FEVER CUCKOO

Hindi: Kapak, Papiha

As the name suggests, the Common Hawk cuckoo or the Brain Fever cuckoo is obstreperous – noisy and difficult to deal with. Herbert Stevens characterises its chorus as 'a pandemonium which reigns all day long throughout the long hours of the night.' Popularly known as *Papiha* in Indian literature, the Brain Fever cuckoo, as the name denotes, does not actually cause a brain fever. It was a name given by the British, for its persistent and, at times, irritating call that goes on endlessly into the night, thus causing a headache.

The papiha too has found a prestigious place in folk songs and Bollywood:

'Bole re papihya, papihaya…

Woh dekho dekh raha hai papiha…

door-papeeha-bola-raat-aadhi-rah-gayi…

Papiha Ke Boliya…'

(Papihaya is calling, papihaya is calling,

From afar it is watching and saying,

The night is already half over,

What then has the papihaya uttered?)

The call of the Brain Fever cuckoo is deeply appreciated in Indian folklore and often figures in Indian erotic poetry. The papiha was also a favourite cage bird and, as mentioned in the Ramayana, was a part of an entourage of pets kept and later released by Sita.

INDIAN ROLLER

Hindi: Neelkanth

Sanskrit: Chaash

The Indian roller or the Neelkanth – meaningly the blue-throated one – is highly revered in Indian mythology and is believed to be the incarnation of Lord Shiva.

THE STORY OF THE SAMUDRA MANTHAN – WHY THE INDIAN ROLLER IS CALLED THE NEELKANTH

During the *Samudra Manthan**, or the churning of the oceans done jointly by the gods and the demons, a pot of poison and amrita – the elixir of life – emerged. The pot of poison was so toxic that it could destroy the whole universe, and it sent a wave of shock, disbelief and fear both amongst the gods and the demons. The gods and the demons pleaded with Lord Vishnu to save the universe from inevitable destruction. Lord Vishnu directed them to Lord Shiva who, according to him, had the sole power to save them. Lord Shiva, out of compassion, was about to drink the poison when Shiva's consort Parvati pressed Shiva's throat to prevent the poison from entering his stomach, thus saving Shiva from any harm. The poison remained in Shiva's throat and turned it blue, hence popularly naming Shiva as Neelkantha or the blue-throated one.

The Indian roller, the Neelkantha or the blue-throated one, is associated and believed to be an incarnation of Lord Shiva. It is, hence, deeply revered in Hindu mythology.

INDIAN ROLLER: MYTHS AND STORIES

Sighting an Indian roller on *Vijaya Dashmi** or *Dussehra* is considered highly auspicious. Ironically, because of this belief, the Indian roller is captured in Northern India – mainly in Uttar Pradesh – worshipped and then released, thus provoking many wildlife enthusiasts to raise voice against the ritual that threatens its very existence.

In another belief, if a person circumambulates a pipal tree on which an Indian roller is perched seven times and the bird gives its blue feather to the worshipper, then the worshipper's wish shall be granted.

INDIAN ROLLER: IN ORNITHOLOGY

In India, we have two species of Rollers, i.e., the Indian roller (*Coracias benghalensis*) and the European roller (*Coracias garrulus*). The Indian roller – a resident species – is found throughout India except for the northern end of Kashmir, while the European roller is a summer visitor to Jammu and Kashmir and North West India, stretching up to Rajasthan and Gujrat.

The Indian roller is also popular for its courtship display by the male birds who perform exquisite aerobatics, rolling and diving upon the female and displaying its collage of colours in flight to entice her.

The mythological status and the beliefs attached to the Indian roller are also threatening its very existence, and the ritual of capturing the bird during *Vijay Dashmi* for enabling worshippers to pay obeisance to Neelkantha must be curbed.

PIGEON AND DOVE

Pigeon - Hindi: Kabootar

Sanskrit: Kanthreev, Paravat, Prasadkukut

Dove - Hindi: Fakhta, Parki, Panduk, Gugi,

Sanskrit: Kapot, Ghugi, Tutroo, Panduk, Parki, Pandukpot

Historically, pigeons and doves were the first of the animal world to be domesticated as early as 3000 BC. Both pigeons and doves belong to the same family *Columbidae* and are morphologically the same. Ornithologists find no behavioural or physical difference between the two. The distinction, if any, is an academic interpretation and should be ignored. Though linguists, as a matter of convention, categorise the larger of the species as 'pigeons' and the smaller ones as 'doves.' Pigeons are monogamous and mate for life. They are portrayed as gentle, romantic and loving. Hence, they are the most appropriate symbols of purity, peace, fertility and matrimonial fidelity. In India, they have a strong symbolic significance and are highly revered by Hindus, Sikhs, Muslims and Christians alike – be it as the reincarnation of departed souls or as symbols of peace. They are universally accepted as symbols of peace.

Pigeon keeping, breeding and flying are prestigious Indian pastimes and were popularised by the Mughal rulers during the medieval period. Even today, it is still a common phenomenon. Many breeds were tailored for exotica, flying, sports and meat. They were developed by the Mughal kings over the centuries, using both indigenous and imported germplasms.

Pigeons are known for their navigation skills and fast flying capabilities. They have been used as messengers and mail carriers. Pigeons have strong homing instincts and are trained to return to their lofts or their source of food. Farmers use pigeon droppings as fertilisers for their crops. During World War II, they were used for guiding missiles onto enemy submarines.

PIGEONS AND DOVES: MYTHS AND STORIES

Pigeons and doves are symbolic of marital fidelity, fertility, love and romance. In Hindu mythology, the pigeon is the favourite and chosen bird of Kamadeva, the god of love. Yama, the god of death, has doves, pigeons and owls as his messengers.

As the legend has it, Tarakasur* – a fiery demon who had unseated Indra as the lord of heavens or *swargalok* – had a boon from Lord Brahma that no one could kill him except for the son born of Shiva's semen. Fearing that if left unchallenged, Tarakasur could create destruction for one and all in the universe, the gods collectively persuaded Goddess Parvati to consummate with Shiva so that the son born of them could neutralise Tarakasur. During the consummation, Agni – the fire god – took the form of a dove to pick the semen of Shiva and discharge it into the Ganga, and from it, the six-headed god Kartikeya was born who went on to kill Tarakasur.

Worshippers sacrifice pigeons during the *Panchbali* ritual along with four other animals, i.e., buffalo, goat, sheep and duck at the Kamkhya temple – dedicated to Kamkhya, the Hindu goddess of sexual desire – in Guwahati in Assam. It is the site of one of the 52 *Shakti Peethas**, where the *yoni* or the vulva of Sati – the consort of Lord Shiva – fell after she sacrificed herself when she and Shiva were insulted by her father, Daksha. The temple is the most respected school of *Tantra*.

IN CHRISTIANITY

The dove is symbolic of the Holy Spirit in Christianity, and it descends upon Jesus at his baptism. It is also portrayed in the pictures of the annunciation, descending on Mary from God as she becomes pregnant with Jesus and shields Mary with its protection.

IN THE LEGEND OF NOAH

In the Old Testament, after the deluge and heavy floods for 40 days, Noah asked the dove to go out from the Ark and search for land. Unable to locate land, the dove was sent out again to search for dry land. After seven days, it returned with an olive branch in its beak as a sign of spotting dry land. Ever since, the dove has symbolised deliverance of God's forgiveness; it represents innocence, simplicity and gentleness and is a symbol of peace and divine guidance.

IN SIKHISM

Sikhs believe that if they feed pigeons, they shall never go hungry when reincarnated. They also feed pigeons because of the belief that pigeons were the known friends of their warrior Guru Govind Singh*.

IN ISLAM

Pigeons are considered holy in Islam as they had come to the rescue of Prophet Mohammed by building a nest and laying eggs at the entrance of the cave where he had taken shelter. His persecutors believed that the birds would never build nests next to human beings, and hence, left the cave untouched, thus saving the Prophet from the clutches of his tormentors.

In 1925, the killing of pigeons by two European boys nearly led to riots in Mumbai, exhibiting the reverence that Muslims have for pigeons.

IN BUDDHISM

Buddhists in Tibet hold pigeons in high reverence. They appear in the lives of *Marpa and Dagmema,* masters of Buddhist Yoga.

One day, *Tarma Doday* – the son of Marpa and Dagmema – had a fatal fall from his horse. As Buddhists believe in reincarnation and the idea that one can transfer the soul from one body to another, *Tarma* – who had earlier learnt the highest form of yoga from his parents – prepared himself after the fall to transfer his soul into another body. While his relatives were frantically searching for a corpse for Tarma to transfer his soul, a hawk that was flying overhead struck a pigeon, and the lifeless pigeon came crashing down on the ground. Marpa immediately collected the lifeless pigeon and placed it on Tarma's body. The pigeon was soon revived and became the carrier of Tarma's soul.

Marpa took charge of the pigeon and nurtured it, while he continued his search through meditation for a suitable alternate human body for Tarma. On receiving a positive sign of the availability of a human body in India, he drew out a map for Tarma – still in pigeon form – and set him off in the air in the direction where the corpse was lying. The pigeon – after a long and distant flight – landed on the chest of the corpse and transferred his soul from the pigeon's body into the human body. People were surprised to see the miracle of the human body coming back to life, and named the boy *Tipupa* – meaning pigeon man in Tibetan.

HOW KING SHIBI WAS PUT TO THE TEST BY THE GODS

King Shibi was a popular ruler in Hindu mythology of the *Chandravamsa* or the Lunar Dynasty, with mentions of him in the Ramayana, Mahabharata and Buddhist Jataka stories. He was a noble, compassionate, generous and charitable king known for being the great protector of the downtrodden.

King Shibi's popularity and compassion for all things living had the gods in heaven both jealous and worried. Agni and Indra colluded and decided to put King Shibi to test. Indra took form as a hawk and went chasing Agni who had taken form as a pigeon. The pigeon (Agni) landed in King Shibi's lap – while he was holding court – and sought his protection. The hawk (Indra) demanded that King Shibi hand over the pigeon to him as the pigeon was his natural food and prey. Shibi refused to do so as the pigeon was now under his protection. Instead, he offered his own flesh, equivalent to the pigeon's weight, as compensation to the hawk. King Shibi put the pigeon on one side of the weighing scales and – much to the distress of the queen and the courtiers – started to cut flesh with a knife from his body to place it on the other side of the scale. With the gods set to test him to the hilt, King Shibi discovered that he could not outweigh the pigeon and stepped on the scale, surrendering his whole body to the hawk. Soon, the hawk and the pigeon disappeared; Agni and Indra made their appearance, complimenting the king for his generosity and blessed him with a boon that he would become a legend and be remembered till time immemorial.

PIGEON KEEPING

Pigeon keeping was a prestigious hobby introduced during the medieval period to the Indian subcontinent by the Mughals with the arrival of Babur*. It was Akbar* who presented Queen Elizabeth I with the first fantail pigeon in the 1600s, and according to his minister Abdul Fazal, Akbar used to travel with over 2,000 pigeons during his journeys.

Pigeon keeping became an integral part of Indian culture, and a dovecote or *chabutras** was a common site in the *havelis** and palaces. It still continues to be a common Indian practice, visible both in urban and rural India, and it is a significant part of Indian traditions and religious beliefs and is practised by followers of all faiths. Traffic islands, large parks and temple compounds in the heart of large metro cities have become popular alternatives to the dovecotes in urban India. On the contrary, feeding pigeons has attained enormous proportions, and many find large flocks of pigeons rather menacing.

PIGEON BREEDING AND FARMING

Like pigeon keeping, pigeon farming too was introduced in the Indian subcontinent during the medieval period by the Mughal kings; it was later taken up as a hobby by the Nawabs of India.

Breeds were developed using both indigenous and imported germplasms. Different varieties of pigeons are bred to meet specific requirements for high- and low-flying pigeons and for utility, i.e., for squabs and meat birds, and for fancy and show purposes. Though there are over 386 different Indian breeds, the common and popular ones are the Geerbaaj, Kalsera, Lalsera, Lal Chhapka, Jeera, Haara, Neelam Kathwa, White Kagdi, Kasni Kanak, Bhathiyara, Udaa, Napta, Bajra, Sulena, Masaal and Taamda. The other popular breeds are Benares and Rajasthan.

PIGEON WARS OR KABUTARBAAZI

Kabutarbaazi is a male-dominated sport that has been practised in India since the 14th century; it is akin to other sports such as cockfighting. Fanciers command their pigeons to fly together in a flock and set them up against enemy flocks over neighbouring rooftops, where they are made to mingle with other unknown enemy flocks. The birds are then manoeuvred into one flock and signalled to return to the home rooftop with the stray pigeons. The owner of the flock whose pigeons join the other flock loses, even if it were just a single pigeon. The captured enemy pigeons are then returned to the original owner after recovery of cost from the contender.

In Lahore, pigeon wars is a popular hobby and regular summer competitions are held in 'Kabutarbaazi.' The participants drug their pigeons and stamp them with 'Lahore' markings on the wings in preparation for the competition. Some of these pigeons stray into surrounding border villages in India, including 'Dauke' Village near Attari in Punjab, where the residents capture, breed and sell them for a profit. Families in Lahore, Pakistan and in bordering Indian villages around Amritsar use pigeons as 'messengers of peace.' They send love messages across both sides of the border through the pigeons, and even feed the famished pigeons that stray into India, treating them as their valued guests from across the border – true to the spirit of *Aman ki Aasha* or the 'Hope for Peace.'

PIGEONS AS MAIL CARRIERS

The Police in the Indian state Orissa, had until recent times, maintained an independent 'P-mail' courier service, using Belgian breed 'homing' pigeons as mail carriers during natural disasters such as floods and famines or during times when modern communication collapsed completely. In one particular instance, in April 1948, Pt. Jawahar Lal Nehru had used the 'Pigeon Mail' services for sending a message to his officials from Sambalpur to Cuttack in Orissa, asking them not to separate the speaker from the audience during his public meeting. The message was correctly delivered in five hours.

HOW PIGEONS NAVIGATE

'Homing' pigeons, a breed having special homing traits, have been used as mail carriers since ancient times by rulers, kings, emperors, nawabs, feudal lords and even armies during World War II, putting to use the 'homing' capabilities that help pigeons to effectively navigate through unfamiliar territories and travel back home hundreds of miles. They use a built-in bio compass in their brain, landmarks, highways, buildings, geomagnetic and 'Sun' orientation as navigational aids and switch from one navigational aid to another depending on the prevailing environmental conditions.

PIGEONS AND DOVES: IN ORNITHOLOGY

Pigeons and doves are amongst the commonest of the birds with over 25 different species found in India. Out of the above, the Blue Rock pigeon *(Columba livia)* is fairly abundant and a familiar sight throughout the Indian countryside and urban surroundings. It lives in semi-domesticated conditions. In many parts of the country, it has come close to being a pest and is even frowned upon. It may be well noted that all the 300 odd domestic breeds originated from the wild rock pigeon. Pigeons and doves are otherwise well-protected and are rarely persecuted because of religious sentiments, and pigeon feeding is a common practice visible across the country.

HORNBILLS

Hindi: Dhanesh

Sanskrit: Matranindak, Priyatmaj, Vayagdhinas

Hornbills are large exotic birds with colourful plumages and prominent overgrown hollow beaks called casques. Primarily tree dwellers, hornbills are frugivorous* and significant dispersers of seeds. They play a critical role in the regeneration of forests.

Known for its elegance, grandiosity, and alertness, the great pied hornbill is highly revered in the North East amongst the tribes in Nagaland and Arunachal Pradesh and is considered as the king amongst the birds by them. It is interlaced with their fables, myths, cultures and folklore. It is depicted in their songs and dances and is manifested in their traditions, faith and costumes. It is considered as a symbol of fertility and strength amongst them. Its feathers, casque and meat are deeply cherished by them and they co-relate their lives with the hornbill's characteristic traits – monogamous life and breeding behaviour, wherein the male hornbill takes over full responsibilities of feeding its partner and the chicks during the period of their house arrest.

It is also a symbol of courage, and the Naga warriors have the privilege of adorning hornbill feathers on their headgears while the beaks of the hornbills are prized by them for valour and manhood. In December every year, tribes from all over Nagaland gather in Kohima to celebrate the annual hornbill festival to pay royal tribute to their cultural icon – the magnificent hornbill. The festival is a cultural feast depicting the lives and culture of the Naga tribes and attracts visitors from across the globe. Old traditions are revived during the festival and the young gather around in the youth dormitories called *morungs,* where the elders pass on their customs and traditions to the next generation. The festival is an extravaganza of art, dance and music during which colourful costumes and headgears are displayed by the youth.

As the tale goes, a distraught youth who suffers at the hands of his stepmother turns into a hornbill and takes flight from his village, promising his beloveds to return every year. On finding his two beloveds married during his one such visit, the jilted Hornbill-youth plucks two feathers from his wings and, after presenting them to each of his beloveds, flies away never to return. The Hornbill feathers now find permanent adornment on the headgears of the tribe and are prominently displayed during the festival.

The Bombay Natural History Society (BNHS) had a resident great hornbill (*Buceros bicornis*) 'William' as its mascot for nearly 26 years. It had lived in a cage behind the Honorary Secretary's chair and had died after swallowing a piece of wire. Later in 1933, it was adopted as the BNHS logo. The official address of the BNHS is also termed as the Hornbill House. The great pied hornbill is also the State Bird of Kerala and Arunachal Pradesh.

Hornbills are known for their exotic plumages, monogamous behaviour and unique nesting habits. They nest in large tree hollows, and the females wall themselves inside a tree hole and seal the entrance from inside with material such as mud, its own droppings and even fruit pulp. They leave a small aperture in the tree hole for the male to feed them during the confinement. The female hornbill's self-confinement lasts till a while after the eggs are laid and hatched. During this intervening period, she is cared for and fed by her devoted mate who makes numerous trips every day to feed her and the chicks with fruits, figs, insects, lizards and small animals. This phenomenon is presumably adopted to protect the nest from predators.

Over nine different species of hornbills are found in India, with the grey hornbill being the commonest and the most widespread of them all. Hornbills use large trees for roosting and nesting and are under great threat due to large-scale felling of trees and loss of forest coverage. The great Indian hornbill is also severely threatened as the tribals of the North East hunt it for its meat. The young birds are considered a delicacy and are also believed to have medicinal properties. Its beak is used as a lucky charm. Hornbill casques are an exotic part of the Naga warriors' headgear, and this part unwittingly contributes to the large-scale culling of the bird. Conservationists have been able to curb the practice by convincing the tribes to replace these with poly fibre and ceramic casques.

MYNAS

Hindi: Myna

Sanskrit: Haholika, Sarika

Belonging to the starling family, mynas figure commonly in Indian literature and folklore right from Vedic times in the Bhagavad Gita, Ramayana, Panchatantra and also in the *Guru Granth Sahib*. The word myna is a local name for most of the starlings in India and is derived from the Hindi and Sanskrit words *maina* and *madana*, meaning delightful and fun-loving.

Mynas are sacred in Hindu mythology, and in India it is widely believed that human souls transmigrate into a Hill Myna (*Gracula religiosa*) after death. They are paraded through the streets on oxen during feast days. Its religious significance in Hindu religion can be further explained, for it helps in the propagation of the Banyan Tree (*Ficus benghalensis*) that is sacred to the Hindus. Hill mynas are also popular as cage birds and are known for their skill in mimicking human speech. They are taught by the Hindus to speak holy and sacred words such as *Ram ram, Ganga ram and Sri Bhagwan*. As mynas pair for life, they are regarded as symbols of everlasting love and fidelity. The Hill myna is the State Bird of Chattisgarh and Meghalaya.

Mynas have been interwoven in Indian culture such that during the tender years of growing up, children had a common belief that spotting a solitary myna meant sorrow while spotting a pair brought joy and happiness.

MYNAS IN SANSKRIT LITERATURE

Mynas have multiple names such as *sarika, kalahpriya, chitranetra, peetanetra* and *peetapaad* in Sanskrit. These names are based more on the habits, traits and physical features that describe it as quarrelsome and argumentative, or as one with picturesque eyes and yellow legs.

It is also known as the *Yagyakunpi* for its notorious pecks at the offerings readied for a religious ceremony, *Parushan*, while the Bank Myna (*Acridotheres ginginianus*) is known as the *Gangsarika* as it breeds on the banks of the River Ganga. The Pied Myna (*Sturnus contra*) is known as *kunpi* for its haughty and scornful nature. The Brahminy Myna (*Sturnus pagodarum*), which has a pleasant song, is considered sacred and auspicious (*Brahminy* meaning sacred in Sanskrit). It is called *gorika* because of its plume. Rosy Pastors (*Sturnus roseus*) that belong to the family of starlings or mynas adorn an attractive black crest and are rose pink in colour are called as *suvarna sarika*, and *madu sarika* because of their love for the nectar that they extract en masse from silk cotton flowers. The Jungle myna (*Acridotheres fuscus*) is called the *Jasht Sarika* because of its dishevelled hair. The name *kalahpriya*, however, is common for all starlings or mynas because of their aggressive and sparring nature.

MYNA: MYTHS AND STORIES

One can pick early lessons on the deceitful ways of the world from the old grandmother's fable in Northern India, where the myna, on the pretext of showing the peacock its dance, deceives the peacock into lending its pretty feet in exchange for its ugly ones and later refuses to return the same. The peacock, who till date retains the ugly feet, sheds tears every time it sees the ugly feet that the myna had deceitfully exchanged.

Mynas also appear with parrots in the Tota–Mynah stories in the *Shukasaptika* stories – a part of katha literature dated back to 12th century AD – where the two birds are projected as lovers and consorts with emphasis laid on their sexual escapades. A similar folklore also exists in neighbouring Nepal where mynas and parrots are considered as consorts. Loving couples are called *Myna justo joda,* while a handsome couple is called as *Myna justo milne* meaning myna-like lovers or myna-like match. Mynas are also considered symbols of fidelity as they mate for life.

THE MYNA IN PANCHATANTRA STORIES

In Panchatantra, the hill myna's skill to mimic human speech, along with that of the parrot, has earned it a reputation, in the poem that aptly describes their traits, and helps us derive some words of wisdom.

The parrots and the myna birds are caged because they utter words; the stupid herons go scot-free for silence is the master-key.

MYNAS AND CROWS

A myna once lost its way to its nest and had to seek shelter on a tree with many crows. Not willing to compromise with their privacy, the crows, despite all pleadings and protests from the myna, forced it to move and seek shelter elsewhere. Soon, the weather changed and down came a heavy rainfall followed by a hailstorm. The myna, taking initiative, found a hole in the tree and took shelter, while the crows preferred to do nothing. In the bargain, many were injured and many were even killed. Later, when the weather cleared, the crows on seeing the myna fly back home asked how she had managed to escape unhurt, to which the myna replied, 'God cares for the humble, while it punishes the proud and the arrogant.'

THE MYNA IN THE PADMA PURANA

The mention of the myna is made in the *Padma Purana*, and it is a part of the story that Lord Shiva narrates to Parvati. A Brahmin's wife *Sarojavadana,* who despite being a devoted wife, was deeply attached to her pet myna and failed to respond to her husband's command; she was then cursed by her husband to become a myna. This myna was adopted by *Muni Kanya*, who – as a part of his rituals – regularly recited the *Tenth Chapter of the Gita* or the '*Vibhuti Yoga Adhyaya*' in which Lord Krishna explains the power of *Vibhuti yoga* to Arjuna. The myna who has the skill to mimic human speech learnt the whole chapter, and in her later birth, became an *apsara**. This apsara was later cursed by Sage Durvasa* into becoming a lotus shrub for having her bath on the banks of a lake on which he too was meditating.

MYNAS OR STARLINGS: IN ORNITHOLOGY

India has eighteen different species of mynas or starlings spread across the subcontinent, and the majority of them are well-adapted to human surroundings, though not all of them can mimic human voices.

The Common Myna (*Acridotheres tristis*), as the generic *Acridotheres* denotes, is a 'grasshopper hunter' and *tristis* in Latin means dull-coloured or the unspotted one. They are one of the most familiar of all the mynas and are omnivorous, though they like to feed on insect and locusts. They are considered friends of the farmers, as they not only help control populations of harmful insects but also help in the pollination of flowers and dispersal of seeds. So extensive is their involvement with humans and their surroundings that they are now considered invasive in some locations.

Hill mynas being excellent mimics of human speech are popular as cage birds, and the pet industry has taken a heavy toll on their numbers. Some incorrigible traders even disguise common mynas by shaving off their eyebrows and painting them orange and yellow. Their bodies are painted with black shoe polish or black grease to pass them off for their cousin, the hill mynas.

FALCONRY IN INDIA

Falconry is a living human heritage and represents multifarious aspects of our culture. For those living in the Indus Valley and the deserts, it was an indispensable instrument for sourcing life-sustaining food. Though the earliest signs of falconry on the Indian subcontinent date back to 600 BC, it was popularised in India by the Mughals. In the later centuries, it became a sport and a noble art practised by those placed in the higher echelons of society. It was a sign of prestige for the aristocrats who were enamoured by the captivating grace and the regality of the raptors.

With the passage of time, falconry continued to remain a practising sport in the region of India, Pakistan and Afghanistan. In India, the royalty in the States of Jaipur and Bhavnagar continued to pursue the sport and patronised it till India achieved freedom. Soon after Independence, the state laws took over, and with the wildlife trade regulations getting rigid and conservationists raising the alarm, falconry was reduced to a dying art and remained only for the sake of academic interest.

The well-known masters of falconry in India were S Mohd. Osman, Late Shantanu Kumar, IPS, Shahid Khan and 'Bazdar' Matekhan Fatehkhan who had served as the hereditary falconer to the Maharajah of Bhavnagar Krishna Kumarsinjhi and his brother R S Dharmakumarsinhji.

THE ART OF FALCONRY

Falconry is an ancient hunting sport where a trained – but not tame – raptor is taught to catch prey in its talons (claws) but not to eat it. Man has held falcons in awe and finds them captivating for being solitary, majestic, royal and individualistic. Falcons prefer to fly freely, intensely searching the countryside with their acute sight and swooping down on their quarry at speeds exceeding 150 to 200 miles an hour. The unforgettable spectacle of the 'tigers of the blue skies' – responding to the call of its master – is an ode to the bondage and respect that exists between the bird and the falconer. In India, the birds were caught in Bhavnagar in Gujarat or sourced from Punjab. Once caught, to calm down the excited falcon, the eyes of the falcon were sealed by slipping a needle through the lower edge of the eyelid and putting the thread over its head. Once the bird loses fear, becomes docile and gets used to human voice and touch, the eyes are unsealed.

The training commences with the trainer tying a lure at the end of a stick and swinging it in front of the falcon, thus inducing it to stoop on the bait. When the falcon gets nearer, the bait is jerked away before the falcon can strike it. After a few attempts, the bird is allowed to strike the bait and allowed to bring down the quarry. With the passage of time, the bird starts responding to the human voice and touch. The bird is rewarded, fed, and then hooded after every training session. Before the commencement of the competition or the hunt, the falcons are drugged to enhance their hunting abilities.

The Indian birds of prey commonly used for falconry are Gowshak, Sparrow Hawk, Shikra, Besra, Peregrine Falcon, Shaheen Falcon, Red Headed Merlin, Lugger Falcon, Saker Falcon, Kestrel, Indian Hobby, Golden Eagle, Bonelli's Hawk Eagle, Crested Hawk Eagle, Changeable Hawk Eagle and even the Common Pariah Kite. Each of the above birds has hunting skills that are unique to its breed, notwithstanding its individual behaviour and personality traits. It is a deep knowledge and intelligent handling of the birds besides the exploitation of their hunting traits by a master falconer that helps convert falconry into a royal and skilful sport.

GLOSSARY

Aakash	One of the five *dhatus* or elements in Hinduism, i.e., Agni (Fire), Aakash (Space), Jal (Water), Vayu (Air) and Prthvi (Earth)
Adi Annamalai Temple	A temple located in Tamil Nadu and dedicated to Lord Shiva. The legend of Adi Annamalai recounts that Brahma, after his dispute with Vishnu about the fiery column, made a lingam and went to establish the Temple of Adi Arunachaleswarar at the village of Adi Annamalai to worship Shiva.
Adi Shankracharya	A philosopher and theologian from India who consolidated the doctrine of Advaita Vedānta in the early 8th Century
Agni	One of the five *dhatus* or elements in Hinduism, i.e., Agni (Fire), Aakash (Space), Jal (Water), Vayu (Air) and Prthvi (Earth). Agni also connotes the Vedic fire god of Hinduism.
Agni Purana	Medieval era encyclopaedia in Sanskrit text. It is one of the eighteen major *Puranas* that covers a diverse range of topics dealing with almost anything and everything.
Akbar	The third and one of the greatest Mughal emperors of the Mughal Dynasty in India. Akbar (1542–1605) succeeded his father, Humayun.

Alakshmi	The older sister of Lakshmi and the Hindu goddess of misfortune. She is also the second wife of Kali, the male demon from the *Kalki Purana* and the Mahabharata.
Amba	Another name for the Hindu Goddess Durga
Amrita	Known to be the elixir of life or the drink of immortality that emerged during the *Samudra manthan* or the churning of the oceans. It is one of the best-known episodes in Hindu mythology. The story appears in the *Bhagavata Purana*, the Mahabharata and the *Vishnu Purana* and explains the origin of amrita.
Angada	A member of the monkey races who helped Rama to find his wife Sita and fight her abductor Ravana in the Ramayana. He was the son of Vali and Tara and the nephew of Sugreeva.
Anthropomorphism	The depiction or treatment of animals, gods, and objects as if they are human
Apsara	Youthful, beautiful and supernatural female beings and experts in the art of dancing in Indian mythology. They are the wives of the *Gandharvas*, the court musicians of Indra.
Aquila	Latin word for eagles and also a genus of birds that includes eagles. It is also an astronomical constellation.
Arboreal	Tree-dwelling animals and birds
Arjuna	One of the principal characters of the ancient Indian epic Mahabharata and plays a key role in the Bhagavad Gita alongside Krishna and is considered to be the best

archer. He was the third of the five Pandava brothers and was married to Draupadi, Ulupi, Chitrangada and Subhadra – Krishna's sister – on different occasions.

Aruna   A mythical bird in Hindu mythology and Surya's charioteer, he is the son of sage Kashyap, brother of Garuda and father of Jatayu and Sampati.

Ashwathama   The son of guru Drona who fought on the Kaurava side against the Pandavas in the epic Mahabharata. The rumours about his death led to the death of Drona– the last commander-in-chief of the Kauravas. He slaughtered many people in the Pandava camp in a sneak attack at night.

Asuras   Powerful superhuman demigods or demons with bad qualities. They are considered to be enemies of the gods in Hindu mythology.

Avadhi   A historical region and present day Lucknow area in Uttar Pradesh, India and is known in British historical texts as Oudh or Oude.

Babur   First Mughal emperor and founder of the Mughal dynasty in the Indian subcontinent. He was a direct descendant of Turco-Mongol conqueror Timur (Tamurlane). He was born in the year 1483.

Bahyakalas   A classical curriculum of "Sixty-four arts" that every married Hindu woman must possess. It includes subjects such as science, arts, dancing, painting, dressing and skills of cultured living listed in various Hindu shastras. Its most well-known appearance is in the *Kama Sutra* – an extensive manual devoted to sensual pleasures.

Baiju Bawara   A legendary dhrupad musician during the Mughal period between 15th and 16th centuries. He was one of the court musicians of Raja Mansingh, Tomar of Gwalior.

Bargadh   A ficus tree (*Ficus bengahalensisis*), it is also called the Bengal tree. It is the national tree of India and considered sacred in Hindu mythology. The leaf of the banyan tree is said to be the resting place of Lord Krishna.

Bhagavad Gita   The Bhagavad Gita is a Hindu scripture in Sanskrit that is part of the Hindu epic Mahabharata and is set in a narrative framework of a dialogue between Pandava prince Arjuna and his guide and charioteer Lord Krishna.

Bhils   Adivasi residents of the Deccan, central and even the far eastern region of India

Bhima   The second of the Pandavas in the Hindu epic Mahabharata and responsible for slaying Duryodhana – the eldest of the Kaurava brothers – in the Kurukshetra War

Bhojpuri   Language spoken in the Bhojpuri region of North India and in Madhesh, Nepal

Brahmastra   A weapon of ultimate destruction against which there was neither any counter-attack nor defence in Hindu mythology. It was believed to be obtained by meditating upon Lord Brahma or from a Guru who knew the invocations.

Brahmin	An aristocratic class that is placed at the top of the hierarchical caste system in Hinduism. They were responsible for the administration of the state, and they played the role of economists and political advisers in the past.
Braj	Also known as Brijbhoomi; it is a region in the state of Uttar Pradesh, India, around the Mathura-Vrindavan. It is considered to be the land of Krishna and is derived from the Sanskrit word *vraja*.
Brij bhasha	The language spoken in the Braj region in Mathura and Brindavan
Brood parasitism	Phenomena observed primarily amongst koels (cuckoos), wherein they invade the nests of other species such as crows and babblers and leave it upon the host bird for incubating and rearing their eggs and chicks.
Brihatkathāmanjari	An ancient Indian epic, it is said to have been written by Guṇaḍhya and is an adaptation of Brihatkathāmanjari by Kshemendra, a Kashmiri philosopher and poet (c. 990 – c. 1070 CE).
Chabutra	A tower-like structure with octagonal- or pentagonal-shaped enclosures at the top. In the upper enclosure, there are several holes, wherein birds can make their nests. It is a structure mostly found at the entrances of villages in Gujarat and Rajasthan, especially for the use of and breeding of pigeons.
Chayyavad	A period in Hindi poetry of the era 1922–1938, marked by an upsurge of romantic and humanist content. It is known for its leaning towards themes of love and nature.

Chidambaram	Located in Tamil Nadu, India and is synonymous with the famous Nataraja Temple dedicated to Lord Shiva, who is depicted as the cosmic dancer, and was built in the Chola era (AD 907 to 1310). Chidambaram is also known for its Bhuvanagiri 'art silk' saris.
Daksha	One of the sons of Lord Brahma who, after creating the ten Manas Putras, created Daksha, Dharma, Kamadeva and Agni from his right thumb, chest, heart and eyebrows respectively, according to Hindu legend. Besides his noble birth, Daksha was also a great king.
Damayanti	A character in a love story found in the *Vana Parva* book of the Mahabharata. She was the princess of Vidharbha Kingdom, who married King Nala of Nishadha Kingdom. She was of such beauty and grace that even the gods could not stop from admiring her. She fell in love with Nala simply by hearing of his virtues and accomplishments from a golden swan.
Darshan	The term for audience granted by gods/ goddesses to their devotees
Devlok	Another name for heaven. In Hindu mythology, it is the abode of the Hindu gods.
Dharmaśāstras	Treatises or the *Shastras* of Hinduism on dharma. There are estimated to be 18 to about 100 Dharmaśāstras.
Dhritrashtra	The King of Hastinapur at the time of the Kurukshetra War in the Mahabharata. Dhritarashtra was blind from birth and

became father to a hundred sons and one daughter by his wife Gandhari. These children, including the eldest son Duryodhana, came to be known as the Kauravas.

Didactic	An action carried out in a manner intended to teach people a moral lesson
Dogri	The language of the Dogras – an Indo-Aryan ethno-linguistic group in India. They live predominantly in the Jammu region of J&K and in adjoining areas of Punjab and Himachal Pradesh.
Dravidians	Native speakers of any of the Dravidian languages of South India. They form the majority of the population of South India.
Drona (or Dronacharya)	The royal preceptor to the Kauravas and Pandavas and an incarnation of Brahma in the Mahabharata. He was a master of advanced military arts, including the divine weapons or astras.
Durbar	A place where Indian kings and other rulers held their formal and informal meetings. In the European context, it is equivalent to a King's Court.
Dushyanta	A king in classical Indian literature and mythology. The story of Dushyanta's encounter, marriage, separation and reunion with his queen, Shakuntala, has been immortalised in Mahabharata and in Kalidasa's play 'Shakuntala' by the great Sanskrit poet Kalidasa.
Dussehra	Also known as Vijayadasami and is an important Hindu festival celebrated in India that marks the victory of Lord Rama

over Ravana. The day also marks the victory of Durga over the demon Mahishasura.

Frugivorous	Fruit-eating birds and animals
Gajendra	Also known as Airavata and is a mythological white elephant who carries the Hindu god Indra. Airavata was born to mother Iravati.
Ganesha	One of the most worshipped deities in Hindu mythology and widely revered as the remover of obstacles. Ganesha's elephant head makes him easy to identify.
Garuda Purana	One of the eighteen *Mahapuranas* that are a vast genre of Indian literature dealing with a wide range of topics, particularly myths, legends and other traditional lore. The text deals with cosmology, mythology, relationships between gods, ethics, good versus evil and various schools of Hindu philosophies.
Gopis	A group of cow herding girls who had unconditional love and devotion to Lord Krishna and Radha
Gurbani	A term commonly used by Sikhs to refer to compositions and hymns of the *Guru Granth Sahib*
Gursikh	A Sikh fully devoted to the true Guru
Guru Govind Singh	The 10th and last of the Sikh Gurus. His four sons died during his lifetime in Muslim-Sikh wars – two in battle and two executed by the Mughal army.
Hanuman	An ardent devotee of Lord Rama. He is one of the central figures in the Hindu epic Ramayana. Hanuman participated in Lord Rama's war against the demon king

	Ravana. Several texts also present him as an incarnation of Shiva. He is the son of Anjana and Kesari and is described as the son of the wind god, Pawan.
Havelis	A term used for traditional townhouses and mansions in India
Hiranyakashyap	An arrogant demon in the old scriptures of Hinduism who thought he was God and demanded that everyone worship only him. He gained magical powers by performing a penance for Lord Brahma. He was subsequently killed by Narasimha – an incarnation of Lord Vishnu.
Indra	The king of the Devas in Hindu mythology. He is the god of lightning, thunder, storms, rains and riverflows. He wields a lightning thunderbolt known as Vajra and rides a white elephant known as Airavata.
Jahangir	Meaning 'conqueror of the world,' he was the fourth of Mughal Emperors and the son of Akbar. Jahangir ruled from the year 1605 until his death in 1627.
Jambuvana	King of the Bears and a character in the Indian epic Ramayana, he helps Rama find his wife Sita and fight her abductor Ravana. It is he who makes Hanuman realise his immense capabilities and encourages him to fly across the ocean in search of Sri Lanka.
Jataka Tales	Stories in Indian literature related to the previous births of Gautama Buddha – both in human and animal form. He appears in them as a king, an outcast, a god and an

	elephant. Each of the tales inculcates and exhibits some virtue.
Kalidasa	A classical Sanskrit writer, he was widely regarded as the greatest poet and dramatist in the Sanskrit language. His well-known works include *Shankuntala* and *Meghdootam*.
Kalptaru tree	A wish-fulfilling divine tree as per Hindu mythology
Kangra	A district in the state of Himachal Pradesh in India
Kansa	A tyrant ruler of Mathura and the brother of Devaki – the mother of Lord Krishna who later slew Kansa in Hindu mythology
Kartikeya	A Hindu god of war and victory and the son of Shiva and Parvati, he is also popularly known as Murugan and Kartik. He has a peacock as his mount.
Kashyapa	An ancient sage who is counted as one of the seven sages or Saptarishis. He is the grandson of Lord Brahma and the son of Marichi. He had many wives; most of them were the daughters of Daksha. In addition to the daughters of Daksha, he also married Syeni, who had a son named Jatayu.
Kauravas	Descendants of Kuru, a legendary king, who is the ancestor of many of the characters of the Mahabharata. The well-known Kauravas are Duryodhana, Dushasana, Vikarna, Yuyutsu and Dussala. They are the children of Dhritarashtra by Gandhari.
King Dasharatha	The king of Ayodhya in the Hindu epic Ramayana. He was a descendant of Raghu

	and was the father of Prince Rama, the principal character in the Ramayana as well as the father of Laxmana, Bharatha and Shatrughna. He had three wives Kaushalya, Sumitra and Kaikeyi.
Krishna	A major Hindu deity and incarnation of Lord Vishnu. Krishna is one of the most widely revered and popular of all Hindu deities.
Kshemendra	A Kashmiri philosopher and poet (c. 990 – c. 1070 CE) and a pupil of Abhinavagupta. He wrote in Sanskrit. Amongst his books is the Brihatkathāmanjari, which is a summary of Gunādhya's Brihatkathā in 7,500 stanzas.
Kumar Gandharva	A renowned Hindustani classical singer (1924 -1992) well known for his unique vocal style
Laxmana	The younger brother of Lord Rama, the hero of the epic and avatar of Lord Vishnu, Laxmana is the twin brother of Shatrughna. He is considered to be an avatar of Shesha Nag, the serpent associated with Vishnu.
Lord Brahma	A part of the Hindu Trinity, along with Vishnu and Shiva, and is the creator god. He has four faces, looking in the four directions and the creator of the four Vedas, one from each of his mouths.
Lord Vishnu	He forms a part of a Hindu trinity along with Brahma and Shiva (Trimurti).
Mahashivratri	A major Hindu festival celebrated annually in honour of Lord Shiva and marks the remembrance of 'overcoming darkness and ignorance' in life.

Manusmriti	A 2nd Century ancient legal text amongst the many Dharmaśāstras of Hinduism. It presents itself as a discourse given by Manu and Bhrigu on dharma topics such as duties, rights, laws, conduct and virtues.
Mayura	The mythological name of the peacock and Lord Kartikeya's mount
Meghalaya	A state in North East India, the name means 'the abode of clouds' in Sanskrit.
Meghdoot or Meghdootam	Meaning cloud messenger, it is a lyric poem written by the great Sanskrit poet Kalidasa.
Meghnad	A prince of Lanka and a conqueror of Indralok (heaven) and the son of King Ravana. As per Ravana's wish, Indrajit was blessed to be a warrior equal to Lord Shiva.
Mirabai	A 16th-century Hindu mystic poetess and devotee of Lord Krishna. She was born to a Rajput royal family in Pali in Rajasthan, India.
Moksha	A term in Hinduism and Hindu philosophy that refers to liberation from the cycle of birth and rebirth
Mulla	An Islamic religious teacher
Murugan	The Hindu god of war and victory, also popularly known as Kartikeya
Nagas	Another name for the serpents
Nagini	A term referring to a female serpent
Narada	A Vedic sage and a devotee of Lord Vishnu who is both wise and mischievous and is famous as a travelling musician and storyteller. He appears in a number of

Hindu texts, notably the Mahabharata and the Ramayana as well as in the mythologies of the Puranas.

Narakasura   The demon son of the earth goddess Bhudevi and Varaha – third incarnation of Vishnu. He was all-powerful and had a long life by virtue of the boon granted to his mother by Vishnu. He later turned his eyes on swargalok and defeated Indra. Narakasura also tried to kill Lord Krishna and was later beheaded by him with his Sudarshana Chakra.

Narsimha   An incarnation of Lord Vishnu. He has a human torso and the face of a lion. Vishnu is believed to have taken this avatar to destroy the demon king Hiranyakashipu.

Padma Purana   One of the eighteen major *Puranas*, a genre of texts of Hindus. It is named after the lotus in which the creator Lord Brahma appeared and includes large sections dedicated to Vishnu, Shiva and Shakti.

Panchatantra   A series of interwoven fables, many of which involve animals exhibiting animal stereotypes. The original Sanskrit work is attributed to Vishnu Sharma and was composed around the 3rd century BC for the benefit of three ignorant princes.

Pandavas   The five acknowledged sons of Pandu by his two wives Kunti and Madri in the Mahabharata. Their names are Yudhishtir, Bhima, Arjuna, Nakula and Sahadeva. All five brothers were married to the same woman, Draupadi.

Papiha   The Hindi name for the Brain Fever cuckoo

Parijat

A flowering tree (*Nyctanthes arbor-tristis* or *Harshingar*). In the *Vishnu Puran*, the Parijat tree appeared as a result of the churning of the oceans. Lord Krishna battled with Indra to win the possession of the Parijat plant. Further on, his wife Satyabhama demanded that the tree be planted in the backyard of her palace. The flowers however used to fall in the adjacent backyard of Lord Krishna's favourite queen Rukmini.

Parvati

The wife of Lord Shiva and the daughter of the mountain king Himavan and Mena. She is the mother of Hindu deities Ganesha and Kartikeya.

Pavolatry

The Peacock Cult, or pavolatry, is a distinctive culture practised by the Dravidians and can be traced back to the Harappan Civilisation.

Pind daan

A ritual performed by Hindus in memory of their departed ancestors. Cooked rice and barley flour balls mixed with ghee and black sesame seeds are immersed in flowing river water as an offering.

Pitr Paksh

A sixteen-day lunar period in the month of September during which Hindus pay obeisance to their departed ancestors. The period is considered inauspicious, and Hindus perform the ritual of *Śrāddha* during which crows are fed with the belief that the food served to them shall be carried to their ancestors in heaven.

Pongal

A four-day harvest festival celebrated by Tamilians in January. The day marks the start of the Sun's six-month-long journey

	northwards – the Uttarayanam. It is primarily celebrated to convey appreciation to the Sun god for providing the energy for agriculture. A part of the celebration is the boiling of the first rice of the season consecrated to the Sun – the Surya Maangalyam.
Pralaya	A period of dissolution or destruction of the Universe at the end of an aeon in Hindu philosophy. Also the end of the world.
Prasad	A Hindi term for a material substance of food that is a religious offering in both Hinduism and Sikhism. It is normally consumed by worshippers after worship.
Puranas	An encyclopaedic genre of Indian literature composed in Sanskrit and covering a wide range of topics, mainly myths, legends and other traditional lore. Several of these texts are named after major Hindu deities such as Vishnu, Shiva and Devi. It includes diverse topics such as cosmology, genealogies of gods, goddesses, kings, heroes, sages and demigods as well as folk tales, pilgrimages, temples, medicine, astronomy, grammar, mineralogy, etc.
Putana	A demoness who was killed by Lord Krishna. Putana tried to kill Krishna when he was still an infant by breastfeeding him with her poisoned milk and was instead killed by Krishna.
Raas leela	The dance of divine love performed by Lord Krishna with Radha and other gopis of Vrindavan. Indian classical dance Kathak

	is known to have originated from the Raas Leela.
Raga	One of the melodic modes used in traditional Indian classical music. Joep Bor of the Rotterdam Conservatory of Music defined raga as tonal framework for composition and improvisation.
Rajdharma	The duties of a ruler that focus on techniques by which one can become an effective and competitive ruler
Rama	The seventh incarnation of the Hindu god Vishnu and the central figure of the Hindu epic Ramayana, which is the principal narration of the events connected to his incarnation on earth, his ideals and his greatness. Rama is one of the many popular deities in Hinduism.
Ramayana	Indian epic ascribed to the Hindu sage Valmiki. The epic narrates the life of Rama, his exile at the behest of his stepmother Kaikeyi from the kingdom by his father, King Dasharatha, his travels across the forests with his wife Sita and brother Laxmana, the kidnapping of his wife by Ravana – the demon king of Lanka – resulting in a war with him and Rama's eventual return to Ayodhya to be crowned as the king. There are many other versions of the Ramayana in Indian languages.
Ravana	The King of Sri Lanka in the Ramayana. He is depicted with ten heads as a follower of Shiva, a great scholar, a capable ruler and a maestro of the veena, but also as someone who wished to overpower the devas. His

	ten heads represent his knowledge of the six shastras and the four Vedas. In the Ramayana, Ravana kidnaps Rama's wife Sita to exact vengeance on Rama and his brother Laxmana for having cut off the nose of his sister Shurpanakha. Ravana is later killed by Rama in a battle to rescue his wife, Sita.
Rig Veda	An ancient Indian collection of Vedic Sanskrit hymns and is one of the four sacred texts of Hinduism known as the *Vedas*
Sage Chyavan	A sage in Hindu mythology who was the son of Bhrigu and is known for his rejuvenation through a special herbal paste known as Chyawanprash, which was first prepared by him
Sage Durvasa	An ancient sage and the son of Atri and Anasuya. He is known for his short temper. Hence, wherever he went, he was received with great reverence from humans and devas alike.
Sage Markandeya	An ancient Hindu sage and a celebrated devotee of both Shiva and Vishnu. He is mentioned in a number of stories from the Puranas.
Sahadeva	The youngest of the five Pandava brothers, i.e., Yudhishtir, Bhima, Arjuna and Nakula
Sampati	Jatayu's brother
Samudra Manthan	Also known as the churning of the ocean, it is one of the best-known episodes in Hindu mythology in which both the gods and the demons participated. The churning of the ocean was an elaborate process and released a number of things from the Ocean of Milk

	including amrita, the elixir of life or the drink of immortality.
Saraswati	The Hindu goddess of knowledge, music, arts, wisdom and learning, and the consort of Brahma – one of the Gods who forms the Trinity along with Vishnu and Shiva.
Satyabhama	The second most important wife of Lord Krishna – the incarnation of Lord Vishnu. Satyabhama is believed to be an avatar of Bhudevi, the earth goddess and consort of Vishnu. She is known for her strong will and tantrums. She aided Krishna in defeating the demon Narakasura.
Shah Jahan	The fifth Mughal emperor of India from 1628 to 1658. Born as Prince Khurram, he was the son of Emperor Jahangir and his Hindu Rajput wife, Taj Bibi Bilqis Makani. Shah Jahan erected many monuments, the best known of which are the Taj Mahal in Agra, the Jama Masjid and the Red Fort at Delhi.
Shakti Peethas	Shrines and pilgrimage centres in Shaktism; historic places of goddess worship in India. As per legend, Lord Shiva enraged and grief-stricken at the death of Goddess Sati roamed around the universe carrying her body. To put an end to Shiva's run, Lord Vishnu used his Sudershana Chakra and dismembered Sati's body into 52 pieces that fell on earth. Each of these spots became major holy spots of worship.
Shakuntala	The wife of King Dushyanta and the mother of Emperor Bharata in Hindu mythology. Her story is told in the Mahabharata and

	dramatised by many writers – the most famous adaptation being Kalidasa's play *Abhijñānaśākuntala*.
Shanidev	Refers to the planet Saturn in Hindu mythology and is one of the nine heavenly objects known as Navagraha in Hindu astrology. Shani is depicted as a male deity whose iconography consists of a dark (black) figure carrying a sword and sitting on a crow.
Shastra	Refers to any treatise, book or instrument of teaching, manual or compendium on any subject in any field of knowledge, including religious ones in Vedic literature
Shiva	One of the principal deities of Hinduism, Shiva is 'the destroyer' within the Trimurti – the Hindu trinity that includes Brahma and Vishnu.
Śrāddha	The ritual that is performed to pay homage to one's 'ancestors,' especially to one's dead parents and to express gratitude towards them and ancestors for having helped them to be what they are, and praying for their peace in Hinduism. It is also a 'day of remembrance.'
Sajaratul Yaakin tree	A large tree that was beyond the seventh heaven in Islam. It is named as *Sidrat al-Muntaha* because all that ascends from earth and whatever descends from heaven terminates here, including divine inspiration that comes down from God.
Sita	The central female character of the Hindu epic Ramayana and daughter of King Janaka and Queen Sunaina. She is the consort of

Lord Rama – an incarnation of Vishnu – and is an avatar of Lakshmi – goddess of wealth and wife of Vishnu. She is known for dedication, self-sacrifice, courage and purity.

Sri Panchamukha
Hanuman

During the war between Lord Rama and Ravana, Hanuman entered pathalalok (hell) in search of Rama and Laxmana. To be able to kill Mahiravana, he had to extinguish five lamps burning in five different directions at the same time. Hanuman took the form of Panchamukha, i.e., Hayagriva, Narasimha, Garuda and Varaha faces and the fifth one being Hanuman himself and extinguished the lamps and killed Mahiravana.

Sugreeva

The younger brother of Vali, whom he succeeded as ruler of the vanara or monkey kingdom of Kishkindha in the Ramayana. He was the son of Surya. As the king of monkeys, Sugreeva aided Rama in his quest to liberate his wife Sita from captivity at the hands of Ravana.

Suparna

Another name of Garuda

Surya

Means the Sun; also connotes the solar deity in Hinduism

Swayamwara

A practice in ancient India where the girl chose her own husband from a list of suitors. On the appointed day and venue, the girl chooses from an assembly of suitors who are required to complete an assigned task. When the girl identifies the husband of her choice, she garlands him and a marriage ceremony is held immediately.

Tamil Nadu	A state in South India
Tantrik	Synonymous in Hinduism to one who practices occult sciences, witchcraft or black magic
Tarakasur	A powerful demon who repeatedly defeated the gods until heaven was on the verge of collapse. He had the boon that he could only be defeated by the son of Shiva. Eventually it was Shiva's son Kartikeya who killed Tarakasur.
Tarpan	Refer 'Pind daan.'
Totem	An object that is respected by a group of people, especially for religious reasons
Tripurasundari	An incarnation of Parvati and the spouse of Kameshwara – a form of Shiva
Uddan khatola	A fictional flying vehicle in the traditional folktales of North India. The term literally means 'flying bedstead' or 'flying cot' but in folklore, the term is used more expansively to cover any flying vehicle.
Upanishads	A collection of texts that contain some of the central philosophical concepts of Hinduism. The *Upanishads* are commonly referred to as Vedānta. The concepts of Brahman – Ultimate Reality – and Atman – Soul, Self – are central ideas in all the Upanishads.
Ustad Mansur	A seventeenth-century Mughal painter and court artist (1590–1624) during the reign of Jahangir. He excelled at depicting plants, animals and natural history illustrations. He was the earliest artist to depict the Dodo in colour and was the first to illustrate the

	Siberian Crane. During the reign of Mughal Emperor Jahangir, his masterpieces earned him the title of *Nādir-al-'Asr* – Unequalled of the age.
Uttar Kand Ramayan	The last chapter of *Ramcharitmanas* is called Uttar Kand, which means that it's actually not a part of the Ramayana, or in the true sense, it is the story of the life and works of Lord Ram. Uttar Kand mostly contains Lord Shiva and Parvati's lives, Kaag Bhusundi's life and the tale of his many previous births.
Vahana	Denotes the being, typically an animal or mythical entity, a particular Hindu deity is said to use as a vehicle. In this capacity, the vahana is often called the deity's 'mount.' The deity may be seen sitting or standing on the vahana.
Valmiki	A poet in Sanskrit literature. The epic 'Ramayana' is attributed to him.
Varsha Ritu	The rainy season in the Hindu calendar
Vasanta Ritu	The spring season in India. One of the main festivals of the Vasanta season is celebrated on Vasanta Panchami.
Vedas	A large body of sacred texts composed in Vedic Sanskrit and originating in the ancient Indian subcontinent; it is also one of the oldest scriptures of Hinduism.
Vibhishana	The younger brother of the demon King Ravana of Lanka in the Ramayana. Vibhishana was a noble character and advised Ravana, who kidnapped and abducted Sita, to return her to her husband, Rama. When Ravana did not listen to his

	advice, Vibhishana joined Rama's army. Later, when Rama defeated Ravana, Rama crowned Vibhishana as the king of Lanka.
Vidharbha	The eastern region of the Indian state of Maharashtra, comprising Nagpur Division and Amravati Division.
Vijaya Dashmi	Also known as *Dussehra* festival
Vinata	The mother of Garuda in Hindu mythology
Vindhya hills	A chain of mountain ridges, hill ranges, highlands and plateau escarpments in west-central India
Yajur Samhita	A part of the ancient Hindu Vedas that dedicates hymns to several ancient deities
Yaksha	The name of a broad class of nature-spirits, usually benevolent, who are caretakers of the natural treasures hidden in the earth and tree roots. They appear in Hindu, Jain and Buddhist texts.
Yudhistira	The eldest of the Pandavas in the epic Mahabharata

BIBLIOGRAPHY

Ali, Salim. *Bird Study in India: Its History and Its Importance.* New Delhi: Indian Council for Cultural Relations, 1979.

Ali, Salim. *The Book of Indian Birds.* Bombay: Bombay Natural History Society, 1941.

Ali, Salim. *The Fall of a Sparrow.* New Delhi: Oxford University Press, 1985.

Ali, Salim and Laeeq Futehally. *Common Birds.* New Delhi: National Book Trust, 1967.

Dave, K. N. *Birds in Sanskrit Literature.* New Delhi: Motilal Banarsidass Publishers, 1985.

Den Besten and Jan Willen. *Birds of Kangra.* Dharamsala: Moon Peak Publishers, 2004.

Grimmett, Richard, Carol Inskipp, and Tim Inskipp. *Birds of the Indian Subcontinent.* Christopher Helm Publishing Company, 2011.

Jackson, Christine E. *Peacock.* London: Reacktion Books, 2006.

Jerolmack, Colin. "Animal Archeology: Domestic Pigeons and the Nature-Culture Dialectic." *Qualitative Sociology Review* 3, no. 1 (April 2007): 74–96. http://www.qualitativesociologyreview. org/ENG/Volume6/QSR_3_1.pdf.

Kazmierczak, Krys. *A Field Guide to the Birds of India, Sri Lanka, Pakistan, Nepal, Bhutan, Bangladesh, and the Maldives.* OM Book Service, 2000.

Krishnan, M. *Of Birds and Birdsong.* Aleph Book Company, 2012.

Marcello, Patricia Cronin. *The Dalai Lama: A Biography.* Greenwood Publishing Group, 2003.

Nair, P. Thankappan. "The Peacock Cult in Asia." *Asian Folklore Studies* 33, no. 2 (1974): 93–170. DOI: 10.2307/1177550.

Naoroji, Rishad. *Birds of Prey of the Indian Subcontinent.* OM Book Service, 2008.

Osman, S. M. *Hunters of the Air: A Falconer's Notes.* WWF India, 1991.

Pande, Satish. *Latin Names of Indian Birds.* New Delhi: Oxford University Press, 2010.

Pande, Suruchi. "Uluka." In *Some Reflections on Birds in Sanskrit Literature,* 44–55. Shodhganga, 2014.

Pattanaik, Devdutt. *7 Secrets of Shiva.* Westland, 2012.

Pattanaik, Devdutt. *7 Secrets of Vishnu.* Westland Books, 2011.

Pattanaik, Devdutt. *99 Thoughts on Ganesha.* Jaico Publishing House, 2013.

Pattanaik, Devdutt. *My Gita.* Rupa Publications, 2015.

Pattanaik, Devdutt. *Myth = Mithya: Decoding Hindu Mythology.* Penguin Books India, 2008.

Siddharth. *The Harlot and the One-eyed Monster.* Leadstart Publishing, 2016.

Singh, Jagjit. *Birds of India.* Books Today, 2001.

Singh, Rajeshwar Prasan Narain. *Bharat Ke Pakshi.* New Delhi: Suchna aur Prasaran Mantralaya.

Singh, Suresh. *Bhartiya Pakshi.* Lucknow, Uttar Pradesh Hindi Sansthan.

Singh, Suresh. *Shikar ke Pakshi.* Lucknow: Hindi Samiti, Suchna Vibhag, Uttar Pradesh Shashan.

Tiwari, J. K and Asad R. Rahmani. "The Common Crane *Grus Grus* and its Habitat in Kutch, Gujarat, India." *Proceedings of the Salim Ali Centenary Seminar* (1996). http://cedobirding. com/Pdf/Common%20Cranes%20and%20its%20 habitat%20in%20Kutch%20JBNHS.pdf.

Urfi, Abdul Jamil. *Birds Beyond Watching.* Universities Press, 2004.

Urfi, Abdul Jamil. *Birds of India: A Literary Anthology.* Oxford University Press, 2010.

Venkatesh, Padmaja. "Place of Symbolism and its Relevance." In *Art of Nātya and the Science of Tantra: A Correlative Study,* 100–3. Shodhganga, 2014.

WWF India. *The Cranes.*

WEB ARTICLES

A. R. Bhatnagar, "12 Divine Names of Bhagwan Garuda (Vehicle of Lord Vishnuji)," last modified in 2010, creative.sulekha. com/12-divine-names-of-bhagwan-garuda-vehicle-of-lord-vishnuji_478096_blog.

Abhilash Rajendran, "Uluka – The Owl as Vahana or Vehicle of Goddess Lakshmi," last modified July 19, 2015, http://www. hindu-blog.com/2009/04/uluka-owl-as-vahana-or-vehicle-of.html.

Ananth Iyer, "Snakes of Indrajit," last modified April 9, 2014, http://talesfrommythology.blogspot.in/search/label/nagpash.

Anthony Jorgensen, "Falcon Facts," http://www.healthguidance. org/entry/15201/1/Falcon-Facts.html.

Anurag Roy, "Importance of Indian National Bird (Peacock)," last modified October 9, 2013, http://www.importantindia. com/2543/importance-of-indian-national-bird/.

Ashutosh Mishra, "Pigeon Mail, a Relic of Past – Technology takes Toll on Oldest Courier Service in State," last modified July 15, 2013, https://www.telegraphindia.com/1130715/jsp/odisha/story_17117192.jsp#.WKffZ9J97IU.

Atula Gupta, "Why Owls of India do not Like Diwali," last modified October 20, 2011, http://indiasendangered.com/why-owls-of-india-do-not-like-diwali/.

"As the Night Bird Chakor Gazes All Night," Sant Mat, last modified February 18, 2014, https://santmat.tumblr.com/post/77109846199/kabir-as-the-night-bird-chakor-gazes-all-night.

Bina Nair, "The Legend of Krishna: Putana Moksham," last modified May 5, 2013, http://vipasana-vidushika.blogspot.in/2013/05/the-legend-of-krishna-putana-moksham.html?view=classic.

"Bird Symbolism and Spiritual Gifts," last modified December 15, 2014, https://exemplore.com/spirit-animals/divine-birds.

Carl Vadivella Belle, "Murugan and the Vel: The Individual Implications," http://murugan.org/research/belle_vel.htm.

Christy Yuncker, "Why do Cranes Dance?" http://www.christyyuncker.com/WhyCranesDance.shtml.

"Celtic Animal Symbols," last modified March 18, 2010, http://symboldictionary.net/?p=942.

"Crane," http://www.catholic-saints.info/catholic-symbols/crane.htm.

"Crane Symbol," http://www.signology.org/bird-symbol/crane-symbol.htm.

D. V. K. Raghavachari, "Modern Hindi Poetry: Its Evolution," http://www.yabaluri.org/CD%20&%20WEB/modernhindipoetryitsevolutionapr53.htm.

Deane Lewis, "Digestion in Owls," last modified on June 19, 2015, http://www.owlpages.com/owls/articles.php?a=4.

Devdutt Pattanaik, "Lakshmi's Owl," http://devdutt.com/articles/indian-mythology/lakshmi%E2%80%99s-owl.html.

"Did the Peacock Throne of the Mogul of India Sink with the Grosvenor?" Look and Learn History Picture Library, last modified December 9, 2013, http://www.lookandlearn.com/blog/28979/did-the-peacock-throne-of-the-mogul-of-india-sink-with-the-grosvenor/.

Federico Lavanche, "A Brief History of Falconry," last modified December 18, 2009, https://www.falconeria.org/a-brief-history-of-falconry/.

Folk Music India, "Dogri Pahari Folk Songs," last modified November 19, 2007, http://dogrimp3.blogspot.in/2007/11/dogri-pahari-folk-songs.html.

Glynn Anderson, "Mynah Birds," last modified in 2009, http://www.garrettphelan.com/Mynah%20Birds%20Glynn%20Anderson%20for%20Garrett%20Phelan.pdf.

"Gopitua Dance History," Gopitua, www.gotipua.com/gotipuadance.html.

"Haṃsa, aka: Hansa, Hamsa, Haṃsā; 15 Definition(s)," Wisdom Library, http://www.wisdomlib.org/definition/ha%E1%B9%83sa.

"History Behind The Peacock Throne | The Greatest Throne Of All Time," Reckon Talk, last modified January 16, 2015, http://www.reckontalk.com/history-behind-the-peacock-throne-the-greatest-throne-of-all-time/.

India Divine, "Immortal Kadamba Tree," last modified December 11, 2012, http://www.indiadivine.org/content/topic/1016077-immortal-kadamba-tree/.

Jaymi Heimbuch, "5 Myths and Superstitions About Owls," last modified May 8, 2015, http://www.mnn.com/earth-matters/animals/blogs/5-myths-and-superstitions-about-owls.

Jeannine Miesle, "Interesting Facts about Members of the Crow Family (Magpies, Crows and Ravens): Intelligence and Adaptations," https://www.beautyofbirds.com/crowintelligence.html.

Jon Lieff, "Only Crows and Humans Can Do It," last modified June 28, 2015, http://jonlieffmd.com/blog/human-brain/only-crows-and-humans-can-do-it.

"Kamakhya: The Mother Goddess," http://www.indiaprofile.com/pilgrimage/kamakhya.htm.

"Legal Issues," Federation of Indian Animal Protection Organisations, http://www.fiapo.org/resources/faqs/legal-issues/.

Madhava Menon, "Varuna – God of the Seas," last modified on March 21, 2008, http://kathaasarit.blogspot.in/2008/03/varuna-god-of-seas.html.

Maseeh Rahman, "Tibetan Crane's Winter Habitat under Threat from Indian Hydroelectric Project," last modified August 27, 2015, https://www.theguardian.com/world/2015/aug/27/tibetan-cranes-winter-habitat-threat-india-hydroelectric-project.

"Mahabharata: Chapter 37," Blessings on the Net, http://blessingsonthenet.com/indianculture/section/articles/185/mahabharata-chapter-thirty-seven.

"Maharishi Valmiki: Composer of Shri Ramayana," Hindu Janajagruti Samiti, https://www.hindujagruti.org/articles/53.html.

"Mayuradhvani - Sound of the Peacock," Blogspot, last modified October 14, 2011, http://muraleeam.blogspot.in/2011/10/mayuradhvani-sound-of-peacock.html.

"Meaning of the Crane," http://www.nzmb.nl/index.php/en/cranes.

"Military Formations in Mahabharata," last modified February 19, 2014, http://www.sanskritimagazine.com/indian-religions/hinduism/military-formations-in-mahabharata/.

"Mystery about Swan: Can it Separate Milk from Water?" last modified on July 6, 2014, https://tamilandvedas.com/2014/07/06/mystery-about-swan-can-it-separate-milk-from-water/.

Oinam Sunil, "At Kamakhya, There's no Stopping Animal Sacrifice," last modified October 16, 2006, http://timesofindia.indiatimes.com/india/At-Kamakhya-theres-no-stopping-animal-sacrifice/articleshow/2172705.cms.

"Owl," http://www.edreaminterpretation.org/owl-3/.

Pooja Gulati, "Why is Peacock the National Bird of India?" last modified September 16, 2006, http://timesofindia.indiatimes.com/home/sunday-times/Why-is-peacock-the-national-bird-of-India/articleshow/1998572.cms.

Premanndhan Narayanan, "What is So Special about Peacock?" last modified November 12, 2012, http://worlddramasecrets.blogspot.in/2012/11/what-is-so-special-about-peacock.html.

"Pigeon Pose," last modified February 15, 2012, http://rexburgyoga.com/blog/?p=942.

Rachna Singh, "Falconry gets UNESCO Recognition," last modified November 3, 2011, http://timesofindia.indiatimes.com/city/jaipur/Falconry-gets-Unesco-recognition/articleshow/10587314.cms.

Ragoo Rao, "A Field Study of the House Sparrow," http://indianwildlifeclub.com/ResearchPapers/Field-Study-of-House-Sparrow.aspx.

Ralph F. Wilson, "Peacock as an Ancient Christian Symbol of Eternal Life," http://www.jesuswalk.com/christian-symbols/peacock.htm.

Shiva Kumar, "The Poor Little Owl…." last modified October 21, 2012, http://www.thehindu.com/sci-tech/energy-and-environment/the-poor-little-owl/article4016944.ece.

Somanath Khuntia, "Sri Krishna and Lord Jagannath," Orissa Review, http://magazines.odisha.gov.in/Orissareview/2009/June/Junereview.htm.

Swami Vimokshananda, "Select Stories from Puranas," last modified December 20, 2015, https://issuu.com/vimoksha/docs/select_stories_from_puranas.

"Shakti Peetham Kamakhya Devi - Uterus of Sati Devi," last modified November 9, 2013, http://indianmandirs.blogspot.in/2013/11/shakti-peetham-kamakhya-devi-uterus-of.html.

"Sparrow: The Chirpy Bird," A Times of India and Forest Department, UP presentation, last modified in 2016.

"Swan," http://www.khandro.net/animal_bird_swan.htm.

"Symbols of the Holy Spirit," Loyola Press, http://www.loyolapress.com/our-catholic-faith/family/catholic-teens/scripture-background-for-teens/symbols-of-the-holy-spirit.

"The Mystique Of The Owl: 10 Strange Myths about Owls," last modified May 15, 2012, http://petslady.com/articles/10_strange_myths_about_owls.

"The Selfish Crows - Panchatantra Story for Kids," http://www.kuttees.in/2013/10/the-selfish-crows-panchatantra-story.html.

"The Swan," The Sikh Foundation International, last modified on January 31, 2011, http://www.sikhfoundation.org/family-corner/birds-animals-of-the-guru-granth-sahib-the-swan/.

"The Tale of the Two Parrots," http://www.indiachildnames.com/stories/the-tale-of-the-two-parrots.html.

"What is the Food of Chakor Bird?" http://www.answers.com/Q/What_is_the_food_of_chakor_bird?#slide=2.

"Why is the Dove Often Used as a Symbol for the Holy Spirit?" https://www.gotquestions.org/Holy-Spirit-dove.html.

"21 Amazing Facts about Pigeons," Pigeon Control Resource Centre, http://www.pigeoncontrolresourcecentre.org/html/amazing-pigeon-facts.html.

WEBSITES

www.amritapuri.org

www.epaper.timesofindia.com

www.goldpix.co

www.indiaprofile.com

www.kamat.com

www.liquisearch.com

www.moef.nic.in

www.quora.com

www.sanatansociety.org

www.speakingtree.in

www.thehindu.com

www.timesofindia.indiatimes.com

www.wikipedia.org

www.ingramcontent.com/pod-product-compliance
Lightning Source LLC
Chambersburg PA
CBHW051451250726
48655CB00001B/354